בָּרוּךְ הַבָּא

Titles in this series:

Just Enough Hebrew

Dror Zeevi

PASSPORT BOOKS
NTC/Contemporary Publishing Group

Dror Zeevi studied for his BA in Middle Eastern history and Semitic linguistics at Tel-Aviv university, going on to attain a PhD in 'The District of Jerusalem in the Seventeenth Century'.

He has given history lectures at both Tel-Aviv and the Hebrew University and was, for three years, the assistant editor of *Zmanim* Historical Quarterly.

He lives in Jerusalem with his wife and three children and is currently doing research at Princeton University, New Jersey.

This edition first published in 1993 by Passport Books,
a division of NTC/Contemporary Publishing Group, Inc.,
4255 West Touhy Avenue,
Lincolnwood (Chicago), Illinois 60712-1975 U.S.A.
Originally published by Pan Books.
Manufactured in the United States of America.
International Standard Book Number: 0-8442-9517-5

10 11 12 13 14 15 QVS/QVS 20 19 18 17 16

Contents

Using the phrase book

- This phrase book is designed to help you get by in Israel, to get what you want or need. It concentrates on the simplest but most effective way you can express these needs in an unfamiliar language.
- The **Contents** on p.v give you a good idea of which section to consult for the phrase you need.
- The **Index** on p.164 gives you more detailed information about where to look for your phrase.
- When you have found the right page you will be given:
  either – the exact phrase
  or – help in making up a suitable sentence
  and – help in getting the pronunciation right.
- The English sentences in **bold type** will be useful to you in a variety of different situations, so they are worth learning by heart. (See also **Do it yourself**, p.157).
- Wherever possible you will find help in understanding what Israeli people say to you in reply to your questions.
- If you want to practise the basic nuts and bolts of the language further, look at the **Do it yourself** section starting on p.157.
- Note especially these three sections:
  Everyday expressions, p.1
  Shop talk, p.57
  You are sure to want to refer to them most frequently.
- Once abroad, remember to make good use of the local tourist offices (see p.18)

  UK address:
  Israel Government Tourist Office
  18 Great Marlborough Street
  London W1

A note on the pronunciation system

There is a great difference between classical, or 'normative' Hebrew, and the way Hebrew is spoken today. Like its Arabic and Aramaic sisters, the written language contains several guttural consonants that are hard to pronounce. But modern spoken Hebrew omits, or softens, most of them. The transcription, therefore, follows the spoken language rather than the written one, and ignores the subtle differences between consonants no longer used.

Travellers' Hebrew offers two transcription systems, plus the original Hebrew:

Hello!   Shalom
                                        shah-*lom*
                                        שלום

The first is a shortened version, based on what most Israelis would view as the right way to write Hebrew in Latin characters. You may find road signs, restaurant menus or pharmacy labels written in the same system. Once you get used to it, you will find it a convenient shorthand.

The second, longer transcription system is not strictly phonetical or scientific. It is intended to enable the English speaker to pronounce the words correctly without any preparation. Here the words are divided into syllables, and the stress in each word is emphasized.

Bear in mind that Hebrew vowels are somewhat flat, and resemble the following examples:

a as in father   (transcribed as ah in open syllables)
e as in bed   (transcribed as eh in open syllables)
i as in sit   (transcribed as ee in open syllables)
o as in opera   (transcribed as oh in open syllables)
u as in put   (here usually transcribed as oo)

The Hebrew alphabet contains a set of consonants which do not appear in Indo-European languages, so many letters do not have equivalents. They are represented by composites of two letters.

א	'	pronounced like the h in hour)
ב	B	
ג	G	(as in ground)
ד	D	
ה	H	(as in home)
ו	V or OO	(van, mOOn)
ז	Z	
ח	H	
ט	T	
י	I or Y	(York, in)
כ	K or Kh	(kite, khutzpe)
ך	K or Kh	(at end of word)
ל	L	
מ	M	
ם	M	(at end of word)
נ	N	
ס	S	
ע	'	(guttural sound)
פ	P and F	(part, full)
ף	F and P	(at end of word)
צ	TS	
ץ	TS	(at end of word)
ק	Q or K	
ר	R	
ש	SH or S	(ship, sip)
ת	T	

The only spoken consonant that does not exist in English is **kh**. It is pronounced as the German nacht, or the Spanish Juan.

Don't forget that Hebrew is read from right to left, and that the beginning of a book or magazine is what appears to Western eyes as the back!

Finally, Israel is an immigrant society. People are used to hearing a variety of accents and pronunciations. Even if your pronunciation is a bit off the mark, people will easily understand.

be-hatslakhah!

Everyday expressions

[See also 'Shop Talk', p.57]

Hello	**shalom** shah-*lom* שלום
Good morning	**Boker tov** *boh*-ker tov בוקר טוב
Good afternoon	**Tsohorayim tovim** tsoh-hoh-*rye*-im toh-*vim* צהריים טובים
Good evening	**Erev tov** *eh*-rev tov ערב טוב
Good night	**Layla tov** *lye*-lah tov לילה טוב
Goodbye	**shalom** shah-*lom* שלום
See you later	**Lehitra'ot** leh-hit-rah-*oht* להתראות
Yes	**Ken** ken כן
Please	**Bevakasha** beh-vah-kah-*shah* בבקשה
Yes, please	**Ken, bevakasha** *ken*, beh-vah-kah-*shah* כן, בבקשה
Great!	**Nehedar** neh-heh-*dahr* נהדר
Thank you	**Toda** toh-*dah* תודה

Thank you very much	**Toda raba** toh-*dah* rah-*bah* תודה רבה
That's right	**Nakhon** nah-*khon* נכון
No	**Lo** loh לא
No, thank you	**Lo toda** loh toh-*dah* לא תודה
I disagree	**Ani lo maskim (m.)/ mas Kimah (f.)** ah-*nee* loh mahs-*kim* (m.)/ mahs-kee-*mah* (f.) אני לא מסכים/מסכימה
Excuse me	**Slakh li** *slakh* li סלח לי
Sorry	**Slikhah** slee-*khah* סליחה
Don't mention it	**ahl lo davar** al loh dah-*vah* על לא דבר
That's OK	**Zeh beseder** zeh beh-*seh*-der זה בסדר
That's good	**Zeh tov** zeh *tov* זה טוב
I like it	**Zeh motseh khen be'eynay** zeh moh-*tseh* khen beh-ehy-*nye* זה מוצא חן בעיני (*lit.* 'It finds grace in my eyes')
That's no good	**zeh lo tov** zeh *loh* tov זה לא טוב
I don't like it	**Zeh lo motseh khen be'eyny** zeh *loh* moh-*tseh* khen beh-ehy-*nye* זה לא מוצא חן בעיני

I know	**Ani yode'a** (m.)/**yoda'at** (f.) ah-*nee* yoh-*deh*-ah (m.)/ yoh-*dah*-aht (f.) אני יודע/ת
I don't know	**Ani lo yode'a** (m.)/**yoda'at** (f.) ah-*nee loh* yoh-*deh*-ah (m.)/ yoh-*dah*-aht (f.) אני לא יודע/ת
It doesn't matter	**Lo khashoov** loh khah-*shoov* לא חשוב
Where's the toilet, please?	**Slikhah, Eyfo ha-sherootim?** slee-*khah, ehy*-foh ha-sheh-roo-*tim* סליחה, איפה השרותים?
How much is that? *[point]*	**kama zeh oleh?** kah-*mah* zeh oh-*leh* כמה זה עולה?
Is the service included?	**Zeh kolel sheroot?** Zeh koh-*lel* sheh-*root* זה כולל שרות?
Do you speak English?	**Ata medaber** (m.)/ **at medaberet** (f.) **anglit?** ah-*tah* meh-dah-*ber* (m.)/ aht meh-dah-*beh*-ret (f.) ahn-*glit* אתה מדבר אנגלית?
I'm sorry	**Ani mitsta'er** (m.)/ **mitsta'eret** (f.) . . . ah-*nee* mits-tah-*ehr* (m.)/ *mits*-tah-*eh*-ret (f.) . . . אני מצטער/ת . . .
I don't speak Hebrew	**ani lo medaber** (m.)/ **medaberet** (f.) **Ivrit** ah-*nee loh* meh-dah-*ber* (m.)/ meh-dah-beh-ret (f.) eev-*rit* אני לא מדבר/תעברית
I only speak a little Hebrew	**ani medaber** (m.)/ **medaberet** (f.) **rak me'at Ivrit** ah-*nee* meh-dah-*ber* (m.)/ meh-dah-*beh*-ret (f.) rahk meh-*aht* eev-*rit* אני מדבר/תרק מעט עברית
I don't understand	**ani lo mevin** (m.)/**mevinah** (f.) ah-*nee loh* meh-*vin* (m.)/ meh-vee-*nah* (f.) אני לא מבין/מבינה

Please can you . . .	**Efshar bevakasha . . .** ehf-*shar* beh-vah-kah-*shah* . . . . . . אפשר בבקשה
repeat that	**lakhzor al zeh** lakh-*zor* ahl *zeh* לחזור על זה
speak more slowly	**ledaber yoter le'at** leh-dah-*ber* yoh-*ter* leh-*at* לדבר יותר לאט
write it down	**likhtov et zeh** leekh-*tov* et *zeh* לכתוב את זה
What is this called in Hebrew? *[point]*	**Ekh kor'im le-zeh be-Ivrit?** ekh kohr-*eem* leh-*zeh* beh-eev-*rit*? איך קוראים לזה בעברית?

Arrival in Israel

ESSENTIAL INFORMATION

- Don't waste time before you leave rehearsing what you're going to say to the border officials – the chances are that you won't have to say anything at all, especially if you travel by air.
- When boarding a flight to Israel you will be asked several routine questions (in English) about your luggage and the purpose of your visit.
- It is useful to check that you have your documents handy for the journey: passport, tickets, money, travellers' cheques, insurance documents, driving licence and car registration documents.
- If you have to give personal details see 'Meeting people' (p.6). The other important answer to know is 'nothing': shoom dah-*vahr*.

ROUTINE QUESTIONS

Passport?	**Darkon?** dahr-*kon* דרכון
Insurance?	**Bituakh?** bee-*too*-ahkh ביטוח

Driving licence?	**Rishyon nehiga?** reesh-*yon* ne-hee-*gah* רשיון נהיגה?
Ticket, please	**Hakartis, bevakasha** ha-kahr-*tiss*, beh-vah-kah-*shah* הכרטיס, בבקשה
Have you anything to declare?	**Yesh lekha toovin le-hatshara?** *Yesh* leh-khah too-*veen* leh-hats-hah-*rah* יש לך טובין להצהרה?
No, nothing	**Lo, shoom davar** *loh*, shoom dah-*vahr* לא, שום דבר
Yes, a few things	**Ken, kama dvarim** *ken*, kah-mah dvah-*rim* כן, כמה דברים
Where are you going?	**Le'an ata nose'a (m.)/ at nosa'at (f.) mikan?** leh-*ahn* at-*tah* no-*seh*-ah (m.)/ noh-sah-aht (f.) mee-*kahn* לאן אתה נוסע/את נוסעת מכאן?
To a hotel in (Jerusalem)	**Le-malon be-(yerooshalayim)** leh-mah-*lon* beh- (yeh-roo-shah-*lah-* yim) למלון בירושלים
To friends in (Haifa)	**Lekhaverim be-(kheyfa)** leh-khah-veh-*rim* be-(khehy-*fah*) לחברים בחיפה
How long are you staying?	**Le-kama zman batem?** leh-*kah*-mah zmahn *bah*-tem לכמה זמן באתם?
A few days	**Kama yamim** *kah*-mah yah-*mim* כמה ימים
A month	**Khodesh** *khoh*-desh חודש
Where have you come from?	**Me'eyfo higaatem?** meh-*ehy*-foh hee-*gaa*-tem מאיפה הגעתם?
Where are you from?	**Me'eyfo atem?** meh-*ehy*-foh ah-*tem*? מאיפה אתם?

Meeting people

[See also 'Everyday Expressions', p.1]

Breaking the ice

Hallo	**Shalom** shah-*lom* שלום
How are you?	**Ma shlomkha? (m.)/** **ma shlomekh? (f.)** mah shlom-*kha* (m.)/ mah-shloh-*mekh*(f.) מה שלומך?
I am well, thank you	**Tov, toda** *tov*, toh-*dah* טוב, תודה
And you?*	**Ve'ata?(m.)/ve'at? (f.)** veh-ah-*ta* (m.)/veh-*aht* (f.) ואתה?/ואת
Pleased to meet you	**Na'im li me'od** nah-*eem* lee me-*ohd* נעים לי מאד
I am here . . .	**Ani kan . . .** ah-*nee* kahn . . . אני כאן . . .
on holiday	**Be-khoofsha** beh-khoof-*shah* בחופשה
on business	**le-asakim** leh-ah-sah-*kim* לעסקים
Would you like . . .*	(m.) **Ata Rotseh . . .** ah-tah roh-*tseh* . . . אתה רוצה . . . (f.) **At Rotsa** aht roh-*tsah* . . . את רוצה . . .
a drink?	**mashehoo lishtot?** *mah*-sheh-hoo lish-*tot* משהו לשתות?

*The personal pronoun **you** has two forms – masculine and feminine. The verbs and adjectives that follow it also change according to the gender.

a cigarette?	**sigarya?**
	see-*gahr*-yah
	סיגריה?
a cigar?	**sigar?**
	sih-*gahr*
	סיגר?

Name

What's your name?	**Mah shimkha?** (m.)/
	mah shmekh? (f.)
	mah sheem-*khah* (m.)/
	mah shmekh (f.)
	מה שמך
My name is . .	**Shmi** . . .
	shmee . . .
	שמי . . .

Family

Are you married?	(m.) **Ata nasooy?**
	ah-*tah* nah-*sooy*
	אתה נשוי?
	(f.) **At nesoo'ah?**
	aht neh-soo-*ah*
	את נשואה?
I am married	(m.) **Ani nasooy**
	ah-*nee* nah-*sooy*
	אני נשוי
	(f.) **Ani nesoo'ah**
	ah-*nee* neh-soo-*ah*.
	אני נשואה
I am single	(m.) **Ani ravak**
	ah-*nee* rah-*vahk*
	אני רווק
	(f.) **Ani ravakah**
	ah-*nee* rah-vah-*kah*
	אני רווקה
This is . . .	(m). **Zeh** . . .
	זה . . .
	(f.) **Zot** . . .
	זאת . . .
my wife	**ishti**
	eesh-*tee*
	אשתי
my husband	**ba'ali**
	bah-ah-*lee*
	בעלי

This is . . .	(m). Zeh . . .	
	. . . זה	
	(f.) Zot . . .	
	. . . זאת	
my son	**bni**	
	bnee	
	בני	
my daughter	**biti**	
	bee-*tee*	
	בתי	
my friend	**khaveri**	
	khah-veh-*ree*	
	חברי	
my colleague	**amiti**	
	ah-mee-*tee*	
	עמיתי	
Do you have any children?	**yesh lekha (m.)/lakh (f.) eladim?**	
	yesh (m.) leh-kha\(f.) lahkh	
	yeh-lah-de	
	ש לך ילדים?	
I have . . .	**Yesh li . . .**	
	yesh lee	
	. . . יש לי	
one daughter	**bat akhat**	
	baht ah-*khaht*.	
	בת אחת	
one son	**ben ekhad**	
	beh eh-*khad*	
	בן אחד	
two daughters	**shtey banot**	
	shtehy bah-*not*.	
	שתי בנות	
three sons	**shlosha banim**	
	shloh-*shah* bah-nim	
	שלושה בנים	
No, I haven't any children	**loh, eyn li yeladim**	
	loh, ehyn lee yeh-lah-*deem*	
	לא, אין לי ילדים	

Where you live

Are you an Israeli?	**Ata yisra'eli? (m.)/**
	at yisraelit? (f.)
	ah-*tah* yis-rah-eh-*lee* (m.)/
	aht yis-rah-eh-*lit* (f.)
	אתה ישראלי?/את ישראלית?

I am English	**Ani angli** (m.)/**angliyah** (f.) ah-*nee* ahn-*glee* (m.)/ ahn-glee-yah (f.) אני אנגלי/ה
I am American *[For other nationalities see p.152]*	**Ani amerika'i** (m.)/**amerika'it** (f.) ah-*nee* ah-meh-ree-*kah*-ee (m.)/ ah-meh-ree-*kah*-it (f.) אני אמריקאי
Where are you from?	**Me'eyfo ata?** (m.)/**at?**(f.) meh-*ehy*-foh ah-*tah* (m.)/aht (f.) מאיפה אתה
I am ...	**Ani ...** ah-*nee*- ... אני
from London	**mi-london** mih-*lohn*-don מלונדון
from England	**me'angliya** meh-*ahn*-glee-yah מאנגליה
from New York	**mi-nyu-york** mee-nyoo-*york* מניו-יורק
from America	**me'amerika** meh-ah-*meh*-ree-kah מאמריקה
from Russia	**me-roosya** meh-*roos*-yah מרוסיה
from the North	**me-hatsafon** meh-hah-tsah-*fohn* מהצפון
from the South	**me-hadarom** meh-hah-dah-*rohm* מהדרום
from the East	**me-hamizrakh** meh-hah-meez-*rakh* מהמזרח
from the West	**me-hama'arav** meh-hah-mah-ah-*rahv* מהמערב

I am . . .	**Ani . . .**
	ah-*nee-*
	. . . אני
from the centre	**me-hamerkaz**
[For other countries,	meh-hah-*mer-kahz*
see p.149]	מהמרכז

For the businessman and woman

I'm from . . . (firm's name)	**Ani meh . . .** (firm's name)
	ah-*nee* meh-(firm's name)
	. . . מ אני
I have an appointment with . . .	**Yesh li pgisha 'im** (person's name)
	yesh lee pghee-*shah* eem (. . .)
	(. . .) יש לי פגישה עם
May I speak to . . .?	**Efshar ledaber 'im . . .** (person's name)?
	ehf-*shahr* leh-dah-*ber* eem (. . .)?
	אפשר לדבר עם (. . .)?
This is my card	**Zeh hakartis sheli**
	zeh hah-kahr-*tiss* sheh-*lee*
	זה הכרטיס שלי
I'm sorry I'm late	**Ani mitsta'er (f. mitsta'eret) al ha'ikhoor**
	ah-*nee* mits-tah-*ehr* (f. mits-tah eh-ret) ahl hah-ee-*khoor*.
	אני מצטער/ת על האיחור
Can I fix another appointment?	**Efshar likbo'a pgisha nosefet?**
	ehf-*shahr* lik-*boh*-ah pgee-*shah* noh-*seh*-fet
	אפשר לקבוע פגישה נוספת?
I'm staying at the (Hilton) hotel	**Ani mitgorer (m.)/ mitgporeret (f.) bemalon (Hilton)**
	ah-*nee* meet-goh-*rehr* (m.)/ meet-goh-*reh*-ret beh-mah-*lohn* (heel-tohn)
	אני מתגורר/ת במלון (הילטון)
I'm staying in (Ben-Yehudah) street	**Ani mitgorer (m.)/ mitgoreret (f.) berekhov Ben-Yehuda**
	ah-*nee* meet-goh-*rehr* (m.)/ meet-goh-*reh*-ret (f.) beh-reh-*khov* (Ben-Yehooda)
	אני מתגורר/ת ברחוב (בן-יהודה)

Asking the way

ESSENTIAL INFORMATION

- Good maps are available for all towns and cities, but new streets are added frequently and old ones change names from time to time.

WHAT TO SAY

Excuse me please	**Slikha** slee-*khah* סליחה
How do I get ...	**Eykh magi 'im ...** eykh mah-ghee-*eem* ... איך מגיעים ...
to Jerusalem?	**le-yerushalayeem?** leh-yeh-rooh-shah-*lah*-yim לירושלים?
to Tel-Aviv?	**le-tel-aviv?** leh-tel-ah-*viv*? לתל-אביב?
to (Nordau) Avenue?	**le-sderot (nordau)?** leh-sdeh-*roht* (nohr-daw) לשדרות נורדאו?
to the (King David) hotel?	**le-malon (hamelekh david)?** leh-mah-*lohn* (hah-*meh*-lekh dah-*vid*) למלון המלך דוד?
to the airport?	**li-sdeh hate'ufah?** lee-*sdeh* hah-teh-oo-*fah* לשדה התעופה?
to the beach?	**le-khof hayam?** leh-*khof* hah-*yahm* לחוף הים?
to the bus station?	**le-takhanat ha'otobus?** leh-tah-khah-*naht* hah-*oh*-toh-boos לתחנת האוטובוס?
to the historic site?	**la-atar hahistori?** lah-ah-*tahr* hah-hiss-*toh*-ree לאתר ההיסטורי?

How do I get . . .

Eykh magi 'im . . .
eykh mah-ghee-*eem* . . .
איך מגיעים . . .

  to the police station?

le-takhanat hamishtara?
leh-tah-khah-*naht* hah-mish-tah-*rah*
לתחנת המשטרה?

  to the port?

la-namal?
lah-nah-*mahl*
לנמל?

  to the (ferry) landing?

la-mezakh?
lah-*meh*-zakh
למזח?

  to the post office?

la-do'ar?
lah-*doh*-ahr
לדואר?

  to the railway station?

le-takhanat harakevet?
leh-tah-khah-*naht* hah-rah-*keh*-vet
לתחנת הרכבת?

  to the sports stadium?

la-itstadyon?
lah-its-tah-*dyohn*
לאיצטדיון?

  to the tourist information office?

le-lishkat hatayarut?
leh-lish-*kaht* hah-tah-yah-*root*
ללשכת התיירות?

  to the town centre?

le-merkaz ha-'ir?
leh-mehr-*kahz* hah-*eer*
למרכז העיר?

  to the town hall?

la-iriya?
lah-eer-*yah*
לעיריה?

Excuse me

Slikha
slee-*khah*
סליחה

Is there . . . nearby?

Yesh kan basvivah . . .
yesh kahn bah-svee-*vah* . . .
יש כאן בסביבה . . .

  an art gallery?

galerya le-omanut?
gah-*lehr*-yah leh-oh-mah-*noot*
גלריה לאמנות?

  a baker's?

ma'afiya?
mah-ah-fee-*yah*
מאפיה?

  a bank?

bank?
bahnk
בנק?

a bar?	**bar?**
	bahr
	בר?
a bus stop?	**takhanat otobus?**
	tah-khah-*naht oh*-toh-boos
	תחנת אוטובוס?
a butcher's	**katsav?**
	kah-*tsahv*
	קצב?
a café?	**bet kafeh?**
	beht kah-*feh*
	בית קפה?
a cake shop?	**konditorya?**
	kohn-dee-*tor*-yah
	קונדיטוריה?
a campsite?	**ma'ahal (or: kemping)?**
	mah-ah-*hull* (kehm-ping)
	מאהל (קמפינג)?
a car park?	**migrash khanaya?**
	meeg-*rahsh* khah-nah-*yah*
	מגרש חניה?
a change bureau?	**khalfan ksafim?**
	khahl-*fahn* ksah-*feem*
	חלפן כספים?
a chemist's	**bet merkakhat?**
	beht mehr-*kah*-khaht
	בית מרקחת?
a church?	**knesiya?**
	kneh-see-*yah*
	כנסיה?
a cinema?	**kolno'a?**
	kohl-*noh*-ah
	קולנוע?
a concert hall?	**'ulam kontsertim?**
	ooh-*lahm* kohn-*tser*-tim
	אולם קונצרטים?
a delicatessen?	**ma'adaniya?**
	mah-ah-dah-nee-*yah*
	מעדניה?
a dentist	**rofeh shinayim?**
	roh-*feh* shee-*nah*-yim
	רופא שיניים?
a department store?	**kol-bo?**
	kohl-boh
	כלבו?

Is there . . . nearby?

Yesh kan basvivah . . .
yesh kahn bah-svee-*vah* . . .
יש כאן בסביבה . . .

  a disco?

    diskotek?
    dis-koh-*tek*
    דיסקוטק?

  a doctor?

    rofeh?
    roh-*feh*
    רופא?

  a dry cleaner's

    nikooy yavesh?
    nee-*kooy* yah-*vesh*
    ניקוי יבש?

  a fishmonger's?

    khanut dagim?
    khah-*noot* dah-*gheem*
    חנות דגים?

  a garage (for repairs)?

    musakh?
    moo-*sahkh*
    מוסך?

  a hairdresser's?

    sapar?
    sah-*pahr*
    ספר?

  a greengrocer's

    yarkan?
    yahr-*kahn*
    ירקן?

  a grocer's

    makolet?
    mah-*koh*-let
    מכולת?

  a hardware shop?

    khanut kley bayit?
    khah-*noot* klehy *bah*-yit
    חנות כלי בית?

  a hospital?

    bet kholim?
    bet khoh-*lim*
    בית חולים?

  a hotel?

    malon?
    mah-*lohn*
    מלון?

  a laundry?

    makhbesa?
    makh-beh-*sah*
    מכבסה?

  a mosque?

    misgad?
    miss-*gahd*
    מסגד?

a museum?	**muzeon?**
	mooh-zeh-*on*
	מוזיאון?
a newsagents?	**khanoot itonim?**
	khah-*noot* ee-toh-nim
	חנות עיתונים?
a nightclub?	**mo'adon layla?**
	moh-ah-*dohn lye*-lah
	מועדון לילה?
a park?	**park?**
	pahrk
	פארק?
a petrol station?	**takhanat delek?**
	tah-khah-*naht deh*-lek
	תחנת דלק?
a postbox?	**tevat do'ar?**
	teh-*vaht* doh-*ahr*
	תבת דואר?
a restaurant	**mis'ada?**
	mees-ah-*dah*
	מסעדה?
a sports ground	**migrash sport?**
	mig-*rush* sport
	מגרש ספורט?
a supermarket?	**supermarket?**
	soo-per-mahr-ket
	סופרמרקט?
a sweet shop?	**khanut mamtakim?**
	khah-*noot* mahm-tah-*kim*
	חנות ממתקים?
a swimming pool	**brekhat skhiya?**
	breh-*khaht* skhee-*yah*
	ברכת שחיה?
a synagogue	**bet kneset?**
	bet *kneh*-set
	בית כנסת?
a taxi stand?	**takhanat moniyot?**
	tah-khah-*naht* moh-nee-*yot*
	תחנת מוניות?
a telephone?	**telefon?**
	teh-leh-fohn
	טלפון?

Is there . . . nearby?	**Yesh kan basvivah . . .**
	yesh kahn bah-svee-*vah* . . .
	. . . יש כאן בסביבה
a theatre?	**te'atron?**
	teh-aht-*rohn*
	תאטרון?
a toilet?	**sherootim?**
	sheh-roo-*tim*
	שרותים?
a travel agent?	**sokhnoot nesi'ot?**
	sokh-*noot* neh-see-*oht*
	סוכנות נסיעות?
a zoo?	**gan khayot?**
	gahn khah-*yot*
	גן חיות?

DIRECTIONS

- Asking where a place is, or if a place is nearby, is one thing; making sense of the answer is another.
- Here are some of the most important key directions and replies.

Left	**Smol**
	smohl
	שמאל
Right	**Yamin**
	yah-*meen*
	ימין
Straight on	**Yashar**
	yah-*shahr*
	ישר
There	**Sham**
	shahm
	שם
First (left/right)	**Harishon (yamina/smola)**
	hah-ree-*shohn* (yah-*mee*-nah/*smoh*-lah)
	הראשון (ימינה/שמאלה)
Second (left/right)	**Hasheni (yamina/smola)**
	hah-sheh-*nee* (yah-*mee*-nah/*smoh* lah)
	השני (ימינה/שמאלה)
At the crossroads	**Batsomet**
	bah-*tsoh*-met
	בצומת

At the roundabout	**Bakikar**
	bah-kee-*kahr*
	בכיכר
At the traffic lights	**Baramzor**
	bah-rahm-*zor*
	ברמזור
It's near	**Zeh karov**
	zeh kah-*rov*
	זה קרוב
It's far	**Zeh rakhok**
	zeh rah-*khok*
	זה רחוק
One kilometre	**Kilometer ekhad**
	ki-loh-*meh*-ter eh-*khahd*
	קילומטר אחד
Two kilometres	**shney kilometer**
	shnehy ki-loh-*meh*-ter
	שני קילומטר
Five minutes . . .	**Khamesh dakot . . .**
	khah-*mesh* dah-*kot*
	חמש דקות . . .
on foot	**ba-regel**
	bah-*reh*-ghehl
	ברגל
by car	**ba-rekhev**
	bah-*reh*-khev
	ברכב
Take . . .	**Kakh . . .**
	kahkh
	קח . . .
the bus	**otoboos**
	oh-toh-boos
	אוטובוס
a cab	**monit**
	noh-*neet*
	מונית
the train	**rakevet**
	rah-*keh*-vet
	רכבת
the ferryboat	**ma'aboret**
	mah-'ah-*boh*-ret
	מעבורת

The tourist information office

ESSENTIAL INFORMATION

- All main towns in Israel and most tourist resort areas have municipal tourist information offices. There are information desks at most airports, train stations and central bus stations. There will usually be someone there who speaks English.
- These offices will give you free information in the form of printed leaflets, fold-outs, brochures, maps, lists and plans.
- For finding a tourist office see p.12.

WHAT TO SAY

Please, have you got . . .	**Slikha, yesh lakhem . . .** slih-*khah*, yesh lah-*khem* . . . . . . סליחה, יש לכם
a plan of the town?	**mapah shel ha-'eer?** mah-*pah* shel hah-*eer* מפה של העיר?
a list of hotels?	**reshimat batey-malon?** reh-shee-*maht* bah-*tehy* mah-*lohn* רשימת בתי מלון?
a list of campsites?	**reshimat kemping?** reh-shee-*maht* *kehm*-ping רשימת קמפינג?
a list of restaurants?	**reshimat mis'adot?** reh-shee-*maht* miss-ah-*doht* רשימת מסעדות?
a list of events?	**tokhnit eroo'im?** tohkh-*neet* eh-roo-*eem* תכנית ארועים?
a leaflet on the town?	**daf hesber al ha-'eer?** dahf hess-*behr* ahl hah-*eer* דף הסבר על העיר?
a leaflet on the region?	**daf hesber al ha-'ezor?** dahf hess-*behr* ahl hah-eh-*zohr* דף הסבר על האזור?
a railway timetable?	**looakh zmaney harakavot?** *loo*-wahkh zmah-*nehy* hah-rah-kah-*voht* לוח זמני הרכבות?

a bus timetable?	**looakh zmaney ha-otobus?** *loo*-wahkh zmah-*nehy* hah-oh-toh-boos לוח זמני האוטובוס?
In English, please	**Be'anglit bevakashah** beh-ahn-*gleet* beh-vah-kah-*shah* באנגלית בבקשה
Can you recommend . . .	**Tookhal lehamlits . . .** too-*khahl* leh-hahm-*lits* . . . תוכל להמליץ . . .
a (cheap) hotel?	**al malon (zol)?** ahl mah-*lohn* (zohl) על מלון (זול)?
a (cheap) restaurant	**al mis'adah (zolah)?** ahl miss-ah-*dah* (zoh-lah) על מסעדה (זולה)?
Can you book a (room/table) for me?	**Tookhloo lehazmin li (kheder/shulkhan)?** tookh-*loo* leh-hahz-*meen* li (*kheh*-dehr/shool-*khahn*) תוכלו להזמין לי (חדר/שולחן)?

LIKELY ANSWERS

Yes	**Ken** kehn כן
Sure	**Betakh** *beh*-tahkh בטח
Why not?	**Lamah lo?** *lah*-mah loh? למה לא?
No	**Lo** loh לא
There isn't/aren't any left	**En yoter** *ehn* yoh-*tehr* אין יותר
I'm sorry	**Mitsta'er** (m.)/**mitsta'eret** (f.) mits-tah-*ehr* (m.)/ mits-tah-*eh*-ret (f.) מצטער/ת

I don't have a list of hotels	**En li reshima shel batey malon**
	ehn lee reh-shee-*mah* shel bah-*tehy* mah-*lohn*
	אין לי רשימה של בתי-מלון
I haven't got any left	**lo nish'aroo li yoter**
	loh nish-ah-*roo* lee yoh-*tehr*
	לא נשארו לי יותר
It's free	**zeh khinam**
	zeh khee-*nahm*
	זה חינם

Accommodations

Hotel

ESSENTIAL INFORMATION

- Most hotels have name boards introducing them in English, as well as Hebrew.
- A list of hotels in town can usually be obtained at the local tourist office.
- Hotels are officially classified into five categories: luxury (five stars), then one to four stars. In small towns, Kibbutzim, etc., there are rooms let on a B&B basis. In most nature resorts there are 'field schools' – hostels providing board and guided tours of the area.
- In most places (all 'official' hotels) the cost is displayed in the room itself, so you can check it when having a look round before agreeing to stay. Usually the costs for breakfast, half board and full board are specified.
- An Israeli breakfast consists of eggs, several salads, several kinds of cheese, bread and jam, fruit, with coffee, chocolate or tea.
- Service is included in the bill unless otherwise specified by notice, but tipping the staff is usual, and will probably provide better service.
- Your passport is requested when registering.
- For finding a hotel see p.11.

WHAT TO SAY

I have a booking	**Hizmanti kheder** hiz-*mahn*-ti *kheh*-der הזמנתי חדר
Have you any rooms, please?	**Ulay yesh lakhem khadarim?** ooh-*lye* yesh la-*khem*, khah-dah-*rim* אולי יש לכם חדרים?
Can I book a room?	**Efshar le-hazmin kheder?** ehf-*shahr* le-hahz-*min kheh*-der אפשר להזמין חדר?
For one person	**Le-adam ekhad** leh-ah-*dahm* eh-*khahd* לאדם אחד

For two people	**Le-shnay anasheem** leh-*shnehy* ah-nah-*sheem* לשני אנשים

(For numbers see p.135]

For ...	**Leh ...** leh ... ל ...
one night	**laylah ekhad** *lye*-lah eh-*khahd* לילה אחד
two nights	**shnay laylot** shnehy lehy-*lot* שני לילות
one week	**shavu'a ekhad** shah-*voo*-ah eh-*khahd* שבוע אחד
two weeks	**shvoo'ayim** shvoo-*ah*-yeem שבועיים
I would like ...	**Ani rotseh (m.)/rotsah (f.) ...** ah-*nee* roh-*tseh* (m.)/roh-*tsah* (f.) אני רוצה ...
a room	**kheder** *kheh*-der חדר
two rooms	**shnay khadarim** *shnehy* khah-dah-*reem* שני חדרים
with a single bed	**'im mitah akhat** eem mee-*tah* ah-*khaht* עם מיטה אחת
with two single beds	**'im shtay mitot nifradot** eem *shtehy* mee-*toht* nif-rah-*doht* עם שתי מיטות נפרדות
with a double bed	**'im mitah kfulah** eem mee-*tah* kfoo-*lah* עם מיטה כפולה
with a toilet	**'im sherootim** eem sheh-roo-*tim* עם שרותים
with a bathroom	**'im ambatya** eem ahm-*baht*-yah עם אמבטיה

with a shower	**'im miklakhat**
	eem meek-*lah*-khat
	עם מקלחת
with a cot	**'im arisa**
	eem ah-ree-*sah*
	עם עריסה
with a balcony	**'im mirpeset**
	eem mir-*peh*-set
	עם מרפסת
Do you serve meals?	**efshar le'ekhol etslekhem?**
	ehf-*shahr* leh-eh-*khohl* ets-leh-*khem*
	אפשר לאכול אצלכם?
At what time is . . .	**matay . . .**
	mah-tye . . .
	. . . מתי
breakfast?	**arookhat haboker?**
	ah-roo-*khaht* hah-*boh*-ker
	ארוחת הבוקר?
lunch?	**arookhat hatsohorayim?**
	ah-roo-*khaht* hah-tso-hoh-*rah*-yim
	ארוחת הצהריים?
dinner?	**arookhat ha'erev?**
	ah-roo-*khaht* hah-*eh*-rev
	ארוחת הערב?
How much is it?	**Kama zeh oleh?**
	kah-mah zeh oh-*leh*
	כמה זה עולה?
Can I look at the room?	**Efshar lir'ot et ha-kheder?**
	ehf-*shahr* lir-*oht* eht hah-*kheh*-der?
	אפשר לראות את החדר?
I'd prefer a room . . .	**Ani ma'adif** (m.)/**ma'adifa** (f.) **kheder . . .**
	ah-*nee* mah-ah-*dif* (m.)/mah-ah-dee-*fah* (m.) *kheh*-der . . .
	. . . אני מעדיף/ מעדיפה חדר
at the front/at the back	**ba-khazit/me-akhor**
	bah-khah-*zeet*/meh-ah-*khor*
	בחזית/מאחור
OK I'll take it	**Tov, ani ekakh oto**
	tov, ah-*nee* eh-*kahkh* oh-*toh*
	טוב, אני אקח אותו

No thanks, I won't take it	**Lo todah, ani lo ekakh oto** loh toh-*dah*, ah-*nee* loh ekahkh oh-*toh* לא תודה, אני לא אקח אותו
The key to number (six) please	**Et hamafte'akh lekheder (shesh) bevakashah** eht hah-mahf-*teh*-akh leh-*kheh*-der (shesh) beh-vah-kah-*shah* את המפתח לחדר (שש) בבקשה
Please may I have . . .	**Efshar lekabel . . .** ehf-*shahr* leh-kah *bel* . . . אפשר לקבל . . .
a coat hanger	**kolav** koh-lahv קולב
a towel	**magevet** mah-*geh*-vet מגבת
a glass	**kos** koss כוס
some soap	**sabon** sah-*bohn* סבון
an ashtray	**ma'afera** mah-ah-feh-*rah* מאפרה
another pillow	**od karit** *ohd* kah-*rit* עוד כרית
another blanket	**od smikhah** ohd smee-*khah* עוד שמיכה
Come in!	**Yavo!** yah-*voh*! יבוא
One moment, please	**Rega ekhad bevakasha** reh-*gah* eh-*khahd* beh-vah-kah-*shah* רגע אחד בבקשה
Please (would you) . . .	**Efshar bevakasha** ehf-*shahr* beh-vah-kah-*shah* אפשר בבקשה

do this laundry	**lekhabes et zeh** leh-khah-*bess* eht *zeh* לכבס את זה
do this dry cleaning	**lenakot et zeh nikooy yavesh** leh-nah-*kot* eht *zeh* nee-*kooy* yah-*vesh* לנקות את זה ניקוי יבש
call me at (six) o'clock	**lehitkasher elay be-(shesh)** leh-hit-kah-*sher* eh-*lye* beh-(shesh) להתקשר אלי בשש
help me with my luggage	**la'azor li 'im hamizvadot** lah-ah-*zor* lee eem hah-miz-vah-*dot* לעזור לי עם המזוודות
call me a taxi for (7) o'clock	**lehazmin li monit lesha'ah (sheva)** leh-hahz-*min* lee moh-*nit* leh-shah-*ah* sheh-vah להזמין לי מונית לשעה (שבע)

[For times, see p.139]

The bill, please	**Hakheshbon bevakasha** hah-khesh-*bohn* beh-vah-kah-*shah* החשבון בבקשה
Is service included?	**Zeh kolel sheroot?** zeh koh-*lel* sheh-*root* זה כולל שרות?
I think this is wrong	**Nidmeh li sheyesh poh ta'oot** nid-*meh* lee sheh-*yesh* poh tah-*oot* נדמה לי שיש פה טעות
May I have a receipt?	**Efshar lekabel kabala?** ehf-*shahr* leh-kah-*bell* kah-bah-*lah* אפשר לקבל קבלה?

At breakfast

Some more . . . please	**Od . . . bevakasha** *ohd* . . . beh-vah-kah-*shah* עוד . . . בבקשה
coffee	**kafeh** kah-*feh* קפה

Some more . . . please	**Od . . . bevakasha**
	ohd . . . beh-vah-kah-shah
	עוד . . . בבקשה
tea	**teh**
	teh
	תה
bread	**lekhem**
	leh-khem
	לחם
butter	**khem'ah**
	khem-*ah*
	חמאה
jam	**reebah**
	ree-*bah*
	ריבה
honey	**dvash**
	dvahsh
	דבש
A boiled egg, please	**Beytsah kashah, bevakasha**
	beh-*tsah* kah-*shah*, beh-vah-kah-*shah*
	ביצה קשה, בבקשה

LIKELY REACTIONS

Can I see your passport, please?	**Efshar lir'ot et hadarkon shelkha (m.)/shelakh (f.) bevakasha?**
	ehf-*shahr* leer-*oht* et hah-dahr-kon shel-*khah*/sheh-*lahkh* beh-vah-kah-*shah*
	אפשר לראות את הדרכון שלך בבקשה?
What's your name?	**Mah shimkhah (m.)/shmekh (f.)?**
	mah shim-*khah*/shmekh
	מה שמך
Sorry, we're full	**Mitsta'er (m.)/mitsta'eret (f.), anakhnoo mele'im**
	mits-tah-*ehr* (m.)/mits-tah-*eh*-ret (f.), ah-*nahkh*-noo meh-leh-*eem*
	מצטער/ת אנחנו מלאים
We have no rooms	**Eyn lanoo khadarim**
	ehn *lah*-noo khah-dah-*reem*
	אין לנו חדרים

Do you want to have a look?	**Aht (f.)/atah (m.)/atem (pl.) rotsim lir'ot otam?** ah-*tem* roh-*tsim* lir-*oht* oh-*tahm* אתם רוצים לראות אותם?
How many people is it for?	**Lekamah anashim?** leh-*kah*-mah ah-nah-shim לכמה אנשים?
From (7) o'clock onwards	**Misha'ah (sheva) ve'eylakh** mee-sha-*ah* (*sheh*-vah) veh-ehy-*lahkh* משעה (שבע) ואילך
From (midday) onwards	**Mehatsohorayim ve'eylakh** meh-hah-tsoh-hoh-*rah*-yim veh-ey-*lahkh* מהצהריים ואילך
[For times, see p.139]	
It's (100) shekels	**Zeh (me'ah) shekel** zeh (meh-*ah*) *sheh*-kel זה (מאה) שקל
[For numbers, see p.135]	

Camping and youth hosteling

ESSENTIAL INFORMATION

Camping

- Look for the word CAMPING, or the Hebrew word קמפינג.
- Many camping sites in Israel are run by the Nature Reserves Authority and have fixed price lists. Others, however, are privately owned and fix their own prices (authorized by the Ministry of Tourism). In many tourist resorts (the Sea of Galilee, the Mediterranean shore, etc.) camping is free of charge and water is provided. Camping off site in very remote places is not advisable.
- You can obtain information on camping sites from local tourist offices, and at any travel agent.

Youth hostels

- Youth hostels can be found in all cities and towns, and in some of the Nature Reserves. Most have shared facilities. An IYHF (International Youth Hostel Federation) card, or a Student card, entitles you to a discount at most hostels.

WHAT TO SAY

I have a booking	**Hizmanti kheder** hiz-*mahn*-tee *kheh*-der הזמנתי חדר
Have you any space?	**Yesh lakhem makom?** yesh lah-*khem* mah-*kom* יש לכם מקום?
It's for ...	**Zeh bishvil ...** zeh bish-vill ... ... זה בשביל
one person	**adam ekhad** ah-*dahm* eh-*khahd* אדם אחד
two people	**shney anasheem** *shnehy* ah-nah-*sheem* שני אנשים
and one child	**veyeled ekhad** veh-*yeh*-led eh-*khahd* וילד אחד

and two children	**veshney yeladim**
	veh-*shnehy* yeh-lah-*dim*
	ושני ילדים
For . . .	**Leh . . .**
	leh . . .
	ל . . .
one night	**laylah ekhad**
	lye-lah eh-*khahd*
	לילה אחד
two nights	**shney leylot**
	snhehy lehy-*lot*
	שני לילות
one week	**shavoo'a ekhad**
	shah-*voo*-ah eh-*khahd*
	שבוע אחד
two weeks	**shvoo'ayim**
	shvoo-*ah*-yim
	שבועיים
How much is it . . .	**Mah hamekhir . . .**
	mah hah-meh-*khir* . . .
	מה המחיר . . .
for the tent?	**le-obel?**
	leh-*oh*-hel
	לאוהל?
for the caravan?	**le-karavan?**
	leh-kah-rah-*van*
	לקרוואן?
for the car?	**le-mekhonit?**
	leh-meh-khoh-*nit*
	למכונית?
for the electricity?	**la-khashmal?**
	lah-khahsh-*mahl*
	לחשמל?
per person?	**le-ish?**
	leh-eesh
	לאיש?
per night?	**le-laylah?**
	leh-*lye*-lah
	ללילה?
May I look around?	**Efshar le-histakel?**
	ehf-*shahr* leh-hiss-tah-*kel*
	אפשר להסתכל?

At what time do you lock up at night?	**Be-eyzo sha'ah atem sogrim ba-laylah?** beh-ehy-*zoh* shah-*ah* ah-*tem* sog-*reem* bah-*lye*-lah באיזו שעה אתם סוגרים בלילה?
Is there anything . . .	**Yesh mashehoo . . .** yesh mah-sheh-hoo . . . . . . יש משהו
to eat?	**le-ekhol?** leh-eh-*khohl* לאכול?
to drink?	**lishtot?** lish-*tot* לשתות?
Is/are there . . .	**Yesh . . .** yesh . . . . . . יש
a bar?	**bar/pub?** bahr/pahb בר/פאב?
hot showers?	**miklakhat khamah?** mik-*lah*-khaht khah-*mah* מקלחת חמה?
a kitchen?	**mitbakh?** mit-bahkh מטבח?
a laundry?	**makhbessa?** mahkh-beh-*sah* מכבסה?
a restaurant?	**mis'adah?** miss-ah-*dah* מסעדה?
a shop?	**khanoot?** khah-*noot* חנות?
a swimming pool	**brekhat skhiya?** breh-*khaht* skhee-*yah* בריכת שחיה?

[For food shopping see p.63,
and for drinking out see p.83]

Where are . . .	**Eyfoh . . .**
	ehy-foh . . .
	. . . איפה
the dustbins?	**pakhey ha-ashpah?**
	pah-*khehy* hah-ahsh-*pah*
	פחי האשפה
the showers?	**hamiklakhot?**
	hah-mik-lah-*khoht*
	המקלחות
the toilets?	**hasherootim?**
	hah-sheh-roo-*tim*
	השרותים
Please have you got . . .	**Oolay yesh lakhem . . .**
	ooh-*lye* yesh lah-*khem* . . .
	אולי יש לכם . . .
a broom?	**matateh?**
	mah-tah-*teh*
	מטאטא
a corkscrew?	**potkhan bakbookim?**
	pot-*khahn* bahk-boo-*kim*
	פותחן בקבוקים
a drying-up cloth	**smartoot ritspah?**
	smahr-*toot* rits-*pah*
	סמרטוט רצפה
a fork?	**mazleg?**
	mahz-*leg*
	מזלג
a fridge?	**mekarer?**
	meh-kah-*rer*
	מקרר
a frying pan?	**makhvat?**
	mahkh-*vaht*
	מחבת
an iron?	**megahets?**
	meh-gah-*hets*
	מגהץ
a knife?	**sakin?**
	sah-*kin*
	סכין
a plate?	**tsalakhat?**
	tsah-*lah*-khaht
	צלחת

Please have you got . . .	**Oolay yesh lakhem . . .**
	ooh-*lye* yesh lah-*khem* . . .
	. . . אולי יש לכם
a saucepan?	**sir?**
	seer
	סיר?
a teaspoon?	**kapit?**
	kah-*pit?*
	כפית?
a tin-opener?	**potkhan kufsa'ot?**
	pot *khahn* koof-sah-*oht*
	פותחן קופסאות?
washing powder	**avkat kvisa?**
	ahv-*kaht* kvee-*sah*
	אבקת כביסה?
washing-up liquid?	**sabon nozli le-kelim?**
	sah-*bohn* nohz-*lee* leh-keh-*lim*
	סבון נוזלי לכלים?
The bill please	**Et hakheshbon bevakasha**
	eht hah-khesh-*bohn* beh-vah-kah *shah*
	את החשבון בבקשה

Problems

The toilet	**Hasherootim**
	hah-sheh-roo-*tim*
	השרותים
The shower	**Hamiklakhat**
	hah-meek-*lah*-khaht
	המקלחת
The tap	**Haberez**
	hah-*beh*-rez
	הברז
The electricity	**Hakhashmal**
	hah-khahsh-*mahl*
	החשמל
The light	**Ha'or**
	hah-*ohr*
	האור
. . . is not working	**lo oved**
	loh oh-ved
	לא עובד

My camping gas has run out	**Balon hagaz sheli nigmar** bah-*lohn* hah-*gahz* sheh-*lee* nig-*mahr* בלון הגז שלי נגמר

LIKELY REACTIONS

May I see your passport please	**Efshar lir'ot et hadarkon shelka (m.)/shelakh (f.) bevakasha?** ehf *shahr* lir-*oht* et hah-dahr-*kon* shel-*khah* (m.)/sheh-lahkh (f.) beh-vah-kah-*shah* אפשר לראות את הדרכון שלך בבקשה?
What's your name	**Mah shimkha (m.)/shmekh (f.)** mah sheem-*khah* (m.) shmehkh (f.) מה שמך?
Sorry, we're full	**Mitsta'er, anakhnoo mele'im** mits-tah-*ehr*, ah-*nahkh*-noo meh-leh-*eem* מצטער, אנחנו מלאים
Do you want to have a look?	**Aht (f.)/atah (m.)/atem (pl.) rotsim lir'ot otam?** ah-*tem* roh-*tsim* lir-*oht* oh-*tahm*? אתם רוצים לראות אותם?
How many people is it for?	**Lekamah anashim?** leh-*kah*-mah ah-nah-*shim* לכמה אנשים?
How many nights is it for?	**Lekama leylot?** leh-kah-*mah* lehy-*loht* לכמה לילות?
It's (50) shekels	**Zeh (khamishim) shekel** zeh (khah-meo-*shim*) *sheh*-kel זה (חמישים) שקל

[For numbers see p.135]

Rented accommodations: problem solving

ESSENTIAL INFORMATION

- For arranging your let see Hotel, p.21.
- Key words you will meet if renting on the spot:
  Khozeh (contract)
  khoh-*zeh*
  Mafte'akh (key)
  mahf-*teh*-ahkh
  Eravon (deposit)
  eh-rah-*vohn*
- When renting accommodation, even for a short while, it is always advisable to sign a contract, specifying the conditions and obligations of both sides.
- Be sure to check the following items:
  Electricity In most cases appliances meet European standards. The voltage is 220v. It is well worth bringing adaptors from home to fit the continental style three-point sockets.
  Cookers are gas operated. Gas is delivered in containers on request. Ask for the gas company's phone number, and for the accommodation's 'client number'.
  Water In most houses a solar water heating system is fitted. Usually the same system can also be heated electrically. Check how to turn on the hot water and how to operate the dual system.
  Equipment For buying or replacing equipment see p.55.
- You will probably have an official agent, but be clear in your own mind whom to contact in an emergency, even if it is only a neighbour in the first place.

WHAT TO SAY

My name is . . .	Shmi . . . shmee . . . שמי . . .
I'm staying at . . .	Ani mitgorer (m.)/mitgoreret (f.) be . . . ah-*nee* mit-goh-*rer* (m.)/ mit-goh-*reh*-ret (f.) beh . . . אני מתגורר/ת ב . . .

The . . . has been cut off	**Hah . . . nootak**
	hah . . . noo-*tahk*
	ה . . . נותק
electricity	**khashmal**
	khahsh-*mahl*
	חשמל
gas	**gaz**
	gahz
	גז
water	**mayim**
	mah-yim
	מים
Is there . . . in the area?	**Yesh . . . basvivah?**
	yesh . . . bah-svee-vah
	יש . . . בסביבה?
an electrician	**khashmala'i**
	khahsh-mah-lah-*ee*
	חשמלאי
a plumber	**shravrav/instalator**
	shrahv-*rahv*/in-stah-*lah*-tor
	שרברב/אינסטלטור
a gas fitter	**tekhna'i gaz**
	tekh-nah-*ee* gahz
	טכנאי גז
Where is . . .	**Eyfo . . .**
	ehy-foh . . .
	איפה . . .
the fusebox?	**aron hakhashmal?**
	ah-*ron* hah-khahsh-*mahl*
	ארון החשמל?
the stopcock? (water main)	**ha-berez ha-rashi?**
	hah-*beh*-rez hah-rah-*shee*
	הברז הראשי?
the boiler?	**ha-dood?**
	hah-*dood*
	הדוד?
the gas tank?	**balon hagaz?**
	bah-*lohn* hah-*gahz*
	בלון הגז

Is there . . .	**Yesh . . .**
	yesh . . .
	. . . יש
central heating?	**hasakah merkazit?**
	hah-sah-*kah* mer-kah-*zeet*
	הסקה מרכזית?
air conditioning?	**mizoog avir?**
	mee-*zoog* ah-*veer*
	מיזוג אוויר?
a lift?	**ma'alit?**
	mah-ah-lit
	מעלית?
bottled gas?	**gaz be-balonim?**
	gahz beh-bah-*loh*-nim
	גז בבלונים?
a telephone?	**telefon?**
	teh-leh-fon
	טלפון?
The cooker	**Ha-kirayim**
	hah-kih-*rah*-yim
	הכיריים
The hair dryer	**Meyabesh ha-se'ar**
	meh-yah-*besh* hah-seh-*ahr*
	מייבש השיער
The heating	**Ha-hasakah**
	hah-hah-sah-*kah*
	ההסקה
The boiler	**Ha-dood**
	hah-*dood*
	הדוד
The iron	**Ha-megahets**
	hah-meh-gah-*hets*
	המגהץ
The pilot light/light bulb	**Ha-noorah**
	hah-noo-*rah*
	הנורה
The refrigerator	**Ha-mekarer**
	hah-meh-kah-*rer*
	המקרר
The washing machine	**Mekhonat ha-kvissah**
	meh-khoh-*naht* hah-kvee-*sah*
	מכונת הכביסה

The telephone	**Ha-telefon** hah-*teh*-leh-fon הטלפון
. . . is not working	**. . . lo oved** loh oh-*vehd* לא עובד
Where can I get . . .	**Eyfo efshar le-hassig . . .** ehy-*foh* ehf-*shahr* leh-hah-*sig* . . . איפה אפשר להשיג . . .
an adaptor for this?	**meta'em le-zeh?** meh-tah-*emn* leh-zeh מתאם לזה?
a bottle of (butane) gas?	**balon gaz (butan)?** bah-*lohn* gahz (boo-*tahn*) בלון גז (בוטאן)?
a fuse?	**pkak khashmali?** pkahk khahsh-mah-*lee* פקק חשמלי?
an insecticide spray?	**sprehy negged kharakim?** spray *neh*-ghed khah-rah-*kim* ספריי נגד חרקים?
a light bulb?	**noorah?** noo-*rah* נורה?
The drain	**Ha-biyoov** hah-bee-*yoov* הביוב
The sink	**Ha-kiyor** hah-kee-*yor* הכיור
The toilet	**Bet ha-shimoosh** beht hah-shee-*moosh* בית השימוש
. . . is blocked	**. . . satoom** sah-*toom* . . . סתום
The gas is leaking	**Ha-gaz dolef** hah-*gahz* doh-*lef* הגז דולף
Can you mend it straight away?	**Tookhal letaken et zeh akhshav?** too-*khahl* leh-tah-*ken* et zeh ahkh-*shahv* תוכל לתקן את זה עכשיו?

When can you mend it?	**Matay tookhal letaken et zeh?** mah-*tye* too-khahl leh-tah-*ken* et zeh מתי תוכל לתקן את זה?
How much do I owe you?	**Kamah ani khayav (m.)/** **khayevet (f.) lekha/lakh?** *kah*-mah ah-*nee* khah-*yahv* (m.)/khah-*yeh*-vet (f.) leh-*kha* (m.)/lahkh (f.) כמה אני חייב/ת לך?
When is the rubbish collected?	**Matay osfim et ha'ashpah?** mah-*tye* oss-*fim* et hah-ahsh-*pah* מתי אוספים את האשפה?

LIKELY REACTIONS

What's your name	**Mah shimkha (m.)/shmekh (f.)?** mah shim-*kha* (m.)/shmekh (f.) מה שמך?
What's your address	**Mah ha-ktovet shelkha (m.)/** **shelakh (f.)?** mah-hah-*ktoh*-vet shel-*khah* (m.)/ sheh-lahkh (f.) מה הכתובת שלך?
There's a shop . . .	**Yesh khanoot . . .** yesh khah-*noot* . . . יש חנות . . .
in town	**ba-'eer** bah-*eer* בעיר
in the village	**ba-kfar** bah-*kfahr* בכפר
I can't come . . .	**Lo 'ookhal lavo . . .** loh ooh-*khahl* lah-*voh* . . . לא אוכל לבוא . . .
today	**hayom** hah-*yohm* היום
this week	**hashavoo'a** hah-shah-*voo*-ah השבוע

until Monday	**ad yom sheni**
	ahd yohm sheh-*nee*
	עד יום שני
I can come ...	**'ookhal lavo ...**
	ooh-*khahl* lah-*voh* ...
	... אוכל לבוא
on Tuesday	**beyom shlishi**
	beh-*yohm* shlee-*shee*
	ביום שלישי
when you want	**matay shetirtseh** (m.)/**shetirtsi** (f.)
	mah-*tye* sheh-tir-*tseh* (m.)/
	sheh-tir-*tsee* (f.)
	מתי שתרצה
every day	**kol yom**
	kol yom
	כל יום
every other day	**pa'am be-yomayim**
	pah-ahm beh-yoh-*mah*-yeem
	פעם ביומיים
on Wednesdays	**biymey revi'i**
	beey-*mehy* reh-vee-*ee*
	בימי רביעי

[For days of the week see p.142]

General shopping

The drugstore / The chemist's

ESSENTIAL INFORMATION

● Look out for this sign.
● Chemists are easy to find, open until 7.00p.m., and in each district take it in turns to stay open throughout the night and during holidays.
Details about the duty chemist in major cities can be found in the information columns of local newspapers.
● Most chemists also sell cosmetics.

● For finding a chemist, see p.13.

WHAT TO SAY

I'd like . . .	**Ani rotseh** (m.) . . ./**rotsah** (f.) . . .
	ah-*nee* roh-*tseh* (m.)/roh-tsah (f.) . . .
	אני רוצה . . .
some aspirin	**aspirin**
	ahs-*pee*-rin
	אספירין
some antiseptic	**khomer khitooy (antisepti)**
	khoh-mer khee-*tooy* (antisepti)
	חומר חיטוי
some bandage	**takhboshet**
	takh-*boh*-shet
	תחבושת
some cotton wool	**tsemer ghefen**
	tseh-mer *gheh*-fen
	צמר גפן
some eye drops	**tipot eynayim**
	tee-*pot* ehy-*nah*-yim
	טיפות עיניים
some foot powder	**avkah la-raglayim**
	ahv-*kah* lah-rahg-*lah*-yim
	אבקה לרגלים
some gauze dressing	**gaza**
	gah-zah
	גזה
some inhalant	**inhalatsya**
	in-hah-*lahts*-yah
	אינהלציה

some insect repellent	khomer dokheh kharakim
	khoh-mer doh-*kheh* khah-rah-*keem*
	חומר דוחה חרקים
some lip salve	mishkhah la-sfatayim
	mish-*khah* lah-sfah-*tah*-yeem
	משחה לשפתיים
some nose drops	tipot af
	tee-*pot* ahf
	טיפות אף
some sticking plaster	plaster
	plah-ster
	פלסטר
some throat pastilles	sookariyot negged shi'ool
	soo-kah-ree-*yot* neh-ghed shee-*ool*
	סוכריות נגד שיעול
some Vaseline	vazelin
	vah-zeh-*leen*
	וזלין
I'd like something for . . .	Ani rotseh (m.) // rotsah (f.)
	mashehu negged . . .
	ah-*nee* roh-*tseh* (m.) / roh-*tsah*
	(f.) *mah*-sheh-hoo *neh*-ghed . . .
	. . . אני רוצה משהו נגד
(insect) bites	akitsot (kharakim)
	ah-kee-*tsot* (khah-rah-*keem*)
	עקיצות (חרקים)
burns/scalds	kviyot
	kvee-*yot*
	כוויות
chilblains	kviyot kor
	kvee-*yot* kor
	כוויות קור
a cold	hitstanenoot
	hits-tah-neh-*noot*
	הצטננות
constipation	atsiroot
	ah-tsee-*root*
	עצירות
a cough	shi'ool
	shee-*ool*
	שיעול
diarrhoea	shilshool
	shil-*shool*
	שילשול

I'd like something for . . .	**Ani rotseh mashehu negged . . .** ah-*nee* roh-*tseh* mah-sheh-hoo *neh*-ghed . . . אני רוצה משהו נגד . . .
earache	**ke'ev oznayim** keh-*ehv* ohz-*nah*-yim כאב אזניים
flu	**shapa'at** shah-*pah*-aht שפעת
sore gums	**ke'ev khanikhayim** keh-*ehv* khah-nee-*khah*-yim כאב חניכיים
sprains	**neka'** *neh*-ka נקע
stings	**akitsot** ah-kee-*tsot* עקיצות
sunburn	**shizoof yeter** shee-*zoof* yeh-ter שיזוף יתר
sea/air/travel sickness	**makhalat yam/avir/derekh** mah-khah-*laht* yahm/ah-*veer*/deh rekh מחלת ים/אוויר/דרך
I need . . .	**Ani tsarikh (m.)/tsrikhah (f.) . . .** ah-*nee* tsah-*reekh* (m.)/ tsree-khah (f.) . . . אני צריך/צריכה . . .
some baby food	**okhel le-tinokot** *oh*-khel leh-tee-noh-*kot* אוכל לתינוקות
some contraceptives	**emtsa'ey meni'ah** ehm-tsah-*ehy* meh-nee-*ah* אמצעי מניעה
some condoms	**kandonim** kahn-*doh*-nim קנדונים
some deodorant	**deodorant** deh-oh-doh-*rahnt* דאודורנט
some disposable nappies	**khitooley niyar** khee-too-*lehy* nee-*yahr* חיתולי נייר

some hand cream	**krem layadayim**
	krehm lah-yah-dah-yim
	קרם לידיים
some lipstick	**lipstick**
	lipstick
	ליפסטיק (שפתון)
some make-up remover	**khomer le-hasarat 'ipoor**
	khoh-mer leh-hah-sah-raht ee-poor
	חומר להסרת איפור
some paper tissues	**mimkhatot niyar**
	meem-kha-tot nee-yahr
	ממחטות נייר
some razor blades	**sakiney gilooakh**
	sah-kee-nehy ghee-loo-ahkh
	סכיני גילוח
some safety pins	**sikot bitakhon**
	see-koht be-tah-khohn
	סיכות ביטחון
some sanitary towels	**takhboshot higyeniyot**
	tahkh-boh-shot heeg-yeh-nee-yot
	תחבושות היגייניות
some shaving cream	**ketsef gilooakh**
	keh-tsehf ghe-loo-akh
	קצף גילוח
some soap	**sabon**
	sah-bohn
	סבון
some suntan lotion (oil)	**krehm (shemen) shizoof**
	krehm (shemen) shee-zoof
	קרם שיזוף
some talcum powder	**talk**
	tahlk
	טלק
some Tampax	**tamponim**
	tahm-poh-nim
	טמפונים
some toilet paper	**niyar toalet**
	nee-yahr toh-ah-let
	נייר טואלט
some toothpaste	**mishkhat shinayim**
	mish-khaht shee-nah-yim
	משחת שיניים

[For other essential expressions see 'Shop talk', p.57]

Holiday items

ESSENTIAL INFORMATION

- Holiday items can be obtained in most supermarkets and stores, especially in the resort areas.
- Many items (including cameras and video) can be rented on a daily basis.

WHAT TO SAY

Where can I buy . . .	Eyfo efshar liknot . . . *ehy*-foh ehf-*shahr* litk-*noht* איפה אפשר לקנות . . .
a bag?	tik? teek תיק?
a beach ball?	kadoor la-yam? kah-*door* lah-*yahm* כדור לים?
a bucket?	dli? dlee? דלי?
an English newspaper?	'iton be-anglit? ee-*tohn* beh-ahn-*gleet* עיתון באנגלית?
some envelopes?	ma'atafot? mah-ah-tah-*fot* מעטפות?
a guide book?	sefer hadrakhah? *seh*-fer hahd-rah-khah ספר הדרכה?
a map?	mapah? mah-*pah* מפה?
some postcards?	glooyot? gloo-*yot* גלויות?
a spade?	ma'ader? mah-ah-*der* מעדר?

a straw hat?	**kova kash?**
	koh-vah kahsh
	כובע קש?
a suitcase?	**mizvadah?**
	meez-vah-dah
	מזוודה?
some sunglasses?	**mishkafey shemesh?**
	meesh-kah-fey sheh-mesh
	משקפי שמש?
a sunshade?	**shimshiya?**
	shim-shee-yah
	שמשיה?
some writing paper?	**niyar ktivah?**
	nee-yahr ktee-vah?
	נייר כתיבה?
I'd like . . . [show the camera]	**Ani rotseh (m.)/**
	rotsah (f.) . . .
	ah-nee roh-tseh (m.)/
	roh-tsah (f.) . . .
	אני רוצה . . .
a colour film	**film tsiv'oni**
	film tsiv-oh-nee
	פילם צבעוני
a black and white film	**film shakhor lavan**
	film shah-khor lah-vahn
	פילם שחור לבן
for prints	**le-tmoonot**
	leh-tmoo-noht
	לתמונות
for slides	**le-shikoofiyot**
	leh-shee-koo-fee-yot
	לשיקופיות
12 (24/36) exposures	**shtem-esreh (esrim ve-arba/shloshim ve-shesh) tmoonot**
	shtehm-ess-reh (ess-rim veh-ahr-bah/shloh-shim veh-shehsh) tmoo-noht
	שתים עשרה (עשרים וארבע/שלושים ושש) תמונות
a video cassette	**kaletet video**
	kah-leh-tet vee-deh-oh
	קלטת וידאו

I'd like . . . *[show the camera]*	**Ani rotseh** (m.)/ **rotsah** (f.) . . . ah-*nee* roh-*tseh* (m.)/ roh-tsah (f.) . . . **אני רוצה . . .**
a standard 8mm film	**seret shmonah milimeter** *seh*-ret shmoh-*nah* mee-lee-*meh*-ter **סרט שמונה מילימטר**
a super 8 film	**seret super shmoneh** *seh*-ret *soo*-per *shmoh*-neh **סרט סופר שמונה**
some flash bulbs	**noorot le-flesh** noo-*roht* leh-*flehsh* **נורות לפלש**
This camera is broken	**Hamatslemah shvoorah** hah-mah-tsleh-*mah* shvoo-*rah* **המצלמה שבורה**
The film is stuck	**Ha-film nitka** hah-*film* nit-*kah* **הפילם נתקע**
Please can you . . .	**Tookhal bevakashah . . .** too-*khahl* beh-vah-kah-*sha* . . . **תוכל בבקשה . . .**
develop this?	**lefateakh et zeh?** leh-fah-*teh*-akh eht-zeh **לפתח את זה?**
print this?	**lehadpis et zeh?** leh-hahd-*piss* eht zeh **להדפיס את זה?**
load the camera?	**lehat'in et hamatslemah?** leh-haht-*een* eht hah-mahts-leh-*mah*? **להטעין את המצלמה?**

[For other essential expressions, see 'Shop talk' p.57]

The tobacco shop

ESSENTIAL INFORMATION

- Although some shops specialize in cigarettes and tobacco, you will usually find these items in general stores and supermarkets, cafés and kiosks.
- Smoking is prohibited in public places, theatres, buses, etc.

WHAT TO SAY

A packet of cigarettes . . .	Koofsat sigaryot . . . koof-*saht* see-*gahr*-yot קופסת סיגריות . . .
with filters	'im filtehr eem *fil*-tehr עם פילטר
without filters	bli filter blee *fil*-tehr בלי פילטר
menthol	mentol mehn-*tohl* מנטול
A packet of kingsize cigarettes	Koofsat sigaryot arookot koof *saht* see-*gahr*-yot ah-roo-*koht* קופסת סיגריות ארוכות
Those over there . . .	Eleh sham . . . *eh*-leh shahm אלה שם . . .
on the right	miyamin mee-yah-*min* מימין
on the left	mismol mee-*smohl* משמאל
These [point]	Eleh *eh*-leh אלה
Cigarettes, please	Sigaryot bevakasha see-*gahr*-yot beh-vah-kah-*shah* סיגריות בבקשה

100/200/300	**Me'ah/maatayim/shlosh-me'ot**
	meh-ah/maah-*tah*-yim/*shlohsh*-meh-*oht*
	מאה/מאתיים/שלוש מאות
Two packets	**Shtey kufsa'ot**
	shtehy koof-sah-*oht*
	שתי קופסאות
Have you got . . .	**Yesh lekha (m.)/lakh (f.) . . .**
	yehsh leh-*khah*/lahkh . . .
	. . . יש לך
English cigarettes?	**Sigaryot angliyot?**
	see-*gahr*-yot ahn-glee-*yoht*
	סיגריות אנגליות?
American cigarettes?	**Sigaryot amerika'iyot?**
	see-*gahr*-yot ah-meh-ree-*kah*-ee yot
	סיגריות אמריקאיות?
English pipe tobacco?	**Tabak angli le-pipe?**
	tah-*bahk* ahn-*glee* leh-pipe
	טבק אנגלי לפייפ?
a packet of pipe tobacco?	**khavilat tabak le-pipe?**
	khah-vee-*laht* tah-*bahk* leh-*pipe*
	חבילת טבק לפייפ?
That one up there . . .	**Zot sham le-ma'ala . . .**
	zoht shahm leh-mah-ah-*lah* . . .
	. . . זאת שם למעלה
on the right	**miyamin**
	mee-yah-*meen*
	מימין
on the left	**mismol**
	mee-*smohl*
	משמאל
That one *[point]*	**Ha-hoo**
	hah-*hoo*
	ההוא
A cigar, please	**Sigar bevakasha**
	see-*gahr* beh-vah-kah-*shah*
	סיגר בבקשה
This one *[point]*	**Zeh**
	zeh
	זה
Some cigars, please	**Kamah sigarim bevakasha**
	kah-mah see-*gah*-rim beh-vah-kah-*shah*
	כמה סיגרים בבקשה

Those *[point]*	**Eleh** *eh*-leh אלה
A box of matches	**Koofsat gafroorim** koof-*saht* gahf-roo-*rim* קופסת גפרורים
A packet of pipe cleaners	**Khavilat menakey pipe** khah-vee-*laht* meh-nah-*kehy* pipe חבילת מנקי פייפ
A packet of flints *[show lighter]*	**Khavilat avanim la-matsit** khah-vee-*laht* ah-vah-*neem* lah-mah-*tseet* חבילת אבנים למצית
Lighter fuel	**Delek lematsitim** *deh*-lek leh-mah-tsee-*tim* דלק למציתים

[For other essential expressions see 'Shop talk', p.57]

Buying clothes

ESSENTIAL INFORMATION

- Clothes measurements fit continental clothing sizes.
- If you are buying for someone else, take their measurements with you.
- See conversion chart of clothing sizes on p.156

WHAT TO SAY

I'd like . . .	**Ani rotseh . . . (m.)/rotsah . . . (f.)** ah-*nee* roh-*tseh* . . . (m.)/roh-tsah . . . (f.) . . . אני רוצה
an anorak	**me'il kham (doobon)** meh-*eel* khahm (doo-*bohn*) (מעיל חם (דובון
a belt	**khagorah** khah-goh-*rah* חגורה
a bikini	**bikini** bee-*kee*-nee ביקיני
a bra	**khaziya** khah-zee-*yah* חזיה
a bathing cap	**kova yam** *koh*-vah yahm כובע ים
a cardigan	**sveder 'im kaftorim** *sveh*-der eem kahf-toh-*rim* סוודר עם כפתורים
a coat	**me'il** meh-*eel* מעיל
a dress	**simlah** sim-*lah* שמלה
a hat	**kova** *koh*-vah כובע

a jacket	**jacket** jah-*ket* ז'קט
a jumper	**sveder** *sveh*-der סוודר
a nightdress	**kootonet laylah** koo-*toh*-net *lye*-lah כותונת לילה
a pullover	**afoodah** ah-foo-*dah* אפודה
some pyjamas	**pijamah** pee-*jah*-mah פיג'מה
a raincoat	**me'il geshem** meh-*eel gheh*-shem מעיל גשם
a shirt	**khooltsah** khool-*tsah* חולצה
a wide brimmed hat	**kova rekhav shoolayim** *koh*-vah reh-*khahv* shoo-*lah*-yim כובע רחב שוליים
a skirt	**khatsa'it** khah-tsah-*eet* חצאית
a suit	**khalifah** khah-lee-*fah* חליפה
a swimsuit	**beged yam** *beh*-ghed yahm בגד ים
some tights	**tights** tights טייטס
some trousers	**mikhnasayim** meekh-nah-*sah*-yim מכנסיים
a T-shirt	**ti-shert** *tee*-shehrt טישרט

I'd like . . .	**Ani rotseh (m.)/rotsah (f.) . . .**
	ah-*nee* roh-*tseh* (m.)/rotsah (f.) . .
	. . . אני רוצה
a pair of briefs/underpants	**takhtonim**
	tahkh-toh-*nim*
	תחתונים
a pair of gloves	**zoog kfafot**
	zoog kfah-*foht*
	זוג כפפות
a pair of jeans	**zoog jins**
	zoog jeens
	זוג ג'ינס
a pair of shorts	**shorts**
	shorts
	שורטס
I'd like a pair of . . .	**Ani tsarikh (m.)/tsrikha (f.) zoog . . .**
	ah-*nee* tsah-*rikh* (m.)/tsree-khah (f.) zoog . . .
	. . . אני צריך זוג
(short/long) socks/stockings	**garbayim (ktsarot/arookot)**
	gahr-*bah*-yim (ktsah-*rot*/ah-roo-*koht*)
	גרביים (קצרות/ארוכות)
shoes	**na'alayim**
	nah-ah-*lah*-yim
	נעליים
canvas shoes	**na'aley bad**
	nah-ah-*lehy* bahd
	נעלי בד
sandals	**sandalim**
	sahn-dah-*lim*
	סנדלים
boots	**magafayim**
	mah-gah-*fah*-yim
	מגפיים
moccasins	**mokasinim**
	moh-kah-*see*-nim
	מוקסינים
slippers	**na'aley bayit**
	nah-ah-*lehy bah*-yit
	נעלי בית
I'd like a pair of beach shoes	**Ani rotseh (m.)/rotsah (f.) zoog na'aley khof**
	ah-*nee* roh-*tseh* (m.)/rotsah (f.) zoog nah-ah-*lehy* khohf
	אני רוצה זוג נעלי חוף

The size is . . .	**Bemidah** . . .
[For numbers see p.135]	beh-mee-*dah* . . .
	. . . במידה
Can I try it on?	**Efshar limdod et zeh?**
	ehf-*shahr* lim-*dohd* eht zeh
	אפשר למדוד את זה?
It's for a present	**Zot matanah**
	zoht mah-tah-*nah*
	זאת מתנה
These are the measurements	**Eleh hamidot**
	eh-leh hah-mee-*dot*
	אלה המידות
bust/chest	**khazeh**
	khah-*zeh*
	חזה
collar	**tsavaron**
	tsah-vah-*rohn*
	צוארון
hip	**yarekh**
	yah-*rekh*
	ירך
leg	**regel**
	reh-ghel
	רגל
waist	**motnayim**
	moht-*nah*-yim
	מותניים
Have you got something . . .	**Yesh lekha** (m.)/**lakh** (f.)
	mashehoo . . .
	yesh leh-*khah*/lahkh *mah*-sheh-hoo . . .
	. . . יש לך משהו
in black?	**beshakhor?**
	beh-shah-*khor*
	בשחור?
in grey?	**be'afor?**
	beh-ah-*for*
	באפור?
in blue?	**bekakhol?**
	beh-kah-*khol*
	בכחול?
in brown?	**bekhoom?**
	beh-*khoom*
	בחום?

Have you got something . . .

Yesh lekha (m.)/**lakh** (f.)
mashehoo . . .
yesh leh-*khah*/lahkh *mah*-sheh-
hoo . . .
יש לך משהו . . .

in pink?	**bevarod?**
	beh-vah-*rod*
	בוורוד?
in green?	**beyarok?**
	beh-yah-*rok*
	בירוק?
in red?	**be'adom?**
	beh-ah-*dom*
	באדום?
in yellow?	**betsahov?**
	beh-tsah-*hov*
	בצהוב?
in this colour?	**batseva hazeh?**
	bah-tseh-vah hah-*zeh*
	בצבע הזה?
in cotton?	**beh-kootnah?**
	beh-koot-*nah*
	בכותנה?
in denim?	**bebad jins?**
	beh-bahd jeens
	בבד ג'ינס?
in leather?	**be'or?**
	beh-*ohr*
	בעור?
in nylon?	**benaylon?**
	beh-*nye*-lohn
	בניילון?
in suede?	**bezamsh?**
	beh-zahmsh
	בזמש?
in wool?	**betsemer?**
	beh-*tseh*-mer
	בצמר?
in this material?	**mehakhomer hazeh?**
	meh-hah-*khoh*-mer hah-*zeh*
	מהחומר הזה?

[For other essential expressions see 'Shop talk' p.57]

Replacing equipment

WHAT TO SAY

Have you got . . .	Yesh lekha (m)/lakh (f) . . .
	yehsh leh-*khah*/lahkh?
	‫. . . יש לך‬
an adaptor?	adaptor?
[show appliance]	ah-*dahp*-tor
	‫אדפטור‬
a bottle of (butane) gas?	balon gaz?
	bah-*lon* gahz
	‫בלון גז‬
a bottle opener?	potkhan bakbukim?
	poht-*khahn* bahk-boo-*kim*
	‫פותחן בקבוקים‬
a corkscrew?	potkhan leyayin?
	poht-*khahn* leh-*yah*-yin?
	‫פותחן ליין‬
any disinfectant?	khomer khitooy?
	khoh-mer khee-*tooy*
	‫חומר חיטוי‬
any paper/plastic cups?	sifley niyar/plastik?
	see-*flehy* nee-*yahr*/*plah*-stik
	‫ספלי נייר/פלסטיק‬
any paper/plastic plates?	tsalakhot niyar/plastik?
	tsah-lah-*khot* nee-*yahr*/*plah*-stik
	‫צלחות נייר/פלסטיק‬
a drying-up cloth?	smartoot ritspah?
	smahr-*toot* rits-*pah*
	‫סמרטוט רצפה‬
any forks?	mazlegot?
	mahz-leh-*got*
	‫מזלגות‬
a fuse [show an old one]	pkak khashmal?
	pkahk khahsh-*mahl*
	‫פקק חשמל‬
an insecticide spray?	sprey neged kharakim?
	sprehy *neh*-ghed khah-rah-*kim*
	‫ספריי נגד חרקים‬

Have you got . . .	**Yesh lekha** (m)/**lakh** (f) . . . yehsh leh-*khah*/lahkh? יש לך . . .
a kitchen roll? *[paper]*	**glil niyar lamitbakh?** gleel nee-*yahr* lah-meet-*bahkh* גליל נייר למטבח?
any knives?	**sakinim?** sah-kee-*nim* סכינים?
a light bulb? *[show old one]*	**nurah?** noo-*rah* נורה?
a plastic bucket?	**dli plastik?** dlee *plah*-stik דלי פלסטיק?
a plug (for the sink)?	**pkak lakiyor?** pkahk lah-kee-*yor* פקק לכיור?
a spanner?	**mafteakh bragim?** mahf-*teh*-ahkh brah-*ghim* מפתח ברגים?
a sponge?	**sfog?** sfohg ספוג?
any string?	**khoot?** khoot חוט?
any tent pegs?	**yetedot le'ohel?** yeh-teh-*dot* leh-*oh*-hel יתדות לאוהל?
a tin-opener?	**potkhan koofsa'ot?** poht-*khahn* koof-sah-*oht* פותחן קופסאות?
a torch?	**panas?** pah-*nahs* פנס?
any (torch) batteries?	**batariyot (le-panas)?** bah-tah-*ree*-yot (leh-pah-*nahs*) בטריות לפנס?
a washing line?	**khevel kvissah?** *kheh*-vel kvee-*sah* חבל כביסה?

any washing powder?	**avkat kvissah?**
	ahv-*kaht* kvee-*sah*
	אבקת כביסה?
a washing-up brush	**mivreshet le-kelim?**
	meev-*reh*-shet leh-keh-*lim*
	מברשת לכלים?
any washing-up liquid?	**sabon nozli le-kelim?**
	sah-*bohn* nohz-li leh-keh-*lim*
	סבון נוזלי לכלים?

[For other essential information, see 'Shop talk', below]

Shop talk

ESSENTIAL INFORMATION

- know your coins and notes:
  coins: 1, 5, 10, 50 Agorah (ah-goh-*rah*)
  1, 5, Shekel (*sheh*-kel) (1 agorah = 0.01 shekel)
  notes: 5, 10, 20, 50, 100 Shekel
- Know how to say the important weights and measures:

50 grams	**Khamishim gram**
	khah-mee-*shim* grahm
	חמישים גרם
100 grams	**Me'ah gram**
	meh-ah grahm
	מאה גרם
½ kilo	**Khatsi kilo**
	khah-*tsi kih*-loh
	חצי קילו
1 kilo	**Kilo**
	kih-loh
	קילו
2 kilos	**Shney kilo**
	shnehy *kih*-loh
	שני קילו
½ litre	**Khatsi liter**
	khah-*tsi lih*-ter
	חצי ליטר

1 litre	**Liter** *lih*-ter ליטר
2 litres	**Shney liter** shnehy *lih*-ter שני ליטר

[For numbers see p.135; for weights and measures conversion tables, see p.154]

CUSTOMER

Hello	**Shalom** shah-*lom* שלום
Good morning	**Boker tov** *boh*-ker tov בוקר טוב
Good afternoon (rarely used)	**Tsohorayim tovim** tsoh-ho-*rah*-yim toh-*vim* צהריים טובים
Good evening	**Erev tov** *eh*-rev *tov* ערב טוב
Goodbye	**Shalom** shah-*lom* שלום
See you later	**Lehitra'ot** leh-hit-rah-*oht* להתראות
Yes	**Ken** ken כן
No	**Lo** loh לא
Please	**Bevakasha** beh-vah-kah-*shah* בבקשה
I'm just looking	**Ani rak mistakel** (m.)/ **mistakelet** (f.) ah-*nee* rahk miss-tah-*kel* (m.)/ miss-tah-*keh*-let (f.) אני רק מסתכל

Excuse me	**Slikhah**
	slee-*khah*
	סליחה
How much is this?	**Kamah zeh oleh?**
	kah-mah zeh oh-*leh*
	כמה זה עולה?
What's that	**Mah zeh?**
	mah zeh
	מה זה?
What are those?	**Mah eleh?**
	mah *eh*-leh
	מה אלה?
Is there a discount?	**Yesh hanakhah?**
	yesh hah-nah-*khah*
	יש הנחה?
I'd like that, please	**Ani rotseh (m.)/**
	rotsah (f.) et zeh, bevakasha
	ah-*nee* roh-*tseh* (m.)/
	roh-tsah (f.) eht zeh beh-vah-kah-*shah*
	אני רוצה את זה, בבקשה
Not that	**Lo zeh**
	loh zeh
	לא זה
Like that	**Kazeh**
	kah-*zeh*
	כזה
That's enough, thank you	**Zeh maspik, todah**
	zeh mahs-*pik*, toh-*dah*
	זה מספיק, תודה
More, please	**Od, bevakashah**
	ohd, beh-vah-kah-*shah*
	עוד, בבקשה
Less than that	**Pakhot mizeh**
	pah-*khot* mee-*zeh*
	פחות מזה
That's fine/OK	**Zeh beseder/OK**
	zeh beh-*seh*-der/oh-kehy
	זה בסדר/אוקיי
I won't take it, thank you	**Ani lo ekakh et zeh, todah**
	ah-*nee* loh eh-*kahkh* et zeh, toh-*dah*
	אני לא אקח את זה, תודה

It's not right	**Zeh lo nakhon**	
	zeh loh nah-*khon*	
	זה לא נכון	
Thank you very much	**Todah rabah**	
	toh-*dah* rah-*bah*	
	תודה רבה	
Is there something . .	**Yesh mashehoo**	
	yesh mah-she-*hoo*	
	יש משהו . . .	
better?	**yoter tov?**	
	yoh-*ter* tohv	
	יותר טוב?	
cheaper?	**yoter zol?**	
	yoh-ter *zohl*	
	יותר זול?	
different?	**shoneh**	
	shoh-*neh*	
	שונה?	
larger?	**yoter gadol?**	
	yoh-*ter* gah-*dohl*	
	יותר גדול?	
smaller?	**yoter katan?**	
	yoh-*ter* kah-*tahn*	
	יותר קטן?	
At what time . .	**Be'eyzeh sha'ah?**	
	beh-*ehy*-zeh shah-*ah*	
	באיזה שעה . . .	
do you open?	**atem potkhim?**	
	ah-*tem* pot-*khim*	
	אתם פותחים?	
do you close?	**atem sogrim?**	
	ah-*tem* sohg-*rim*	
	אתם סוגרים?	
Can I have a bag, please?	**Efshar lekabel sakit, bevakashah?**	
	ehf-shahr leh-kah-*bel* sah-*kit*, beh-vah-kah-*shah*	
	אפשר לקבל שקית, בבקשה?	
Can I have a receipt?	**Efshar lekabel kabalah?**	
	ehf-*shahr* leh-kah-*bel* kah-bah-*lah*	
	אפשר לקבל קבלה?	

Do you take . . .	**Atem mekablim . . .**
	ah-*tem* meh-kabb-*lim* . . .
	. . . אתם מקבלים
English/American money?	**kessef angli/amerika'l?**
	keh-sef ahn-*gli*/ah-meh-ree-*kah*-ee
	כסף אנגלי/אמריקאי?
travellers' cheques?	**travelers cheks?**
	trah-veh-lers cheks
	טראבלרס צ'קס (המחאות נוסעים)?
credit cards?	**kartisey ashray?**
	kahr-tee-*sehy* ahsh-*rye*
	כרטיסי אשראי?
I'd like . . .	**Ani rotseh (m.)/**
	rotsah (f.) . . .
	ah-*nee* roht-*seh* (m.)/
	roht-tsah (f.) . . .
	. . . אני רוצה
one like that	**ekhad kazeh**
	eh-*khahd* kah-*zeh*
	אחד כזה
two like that	**shnayim ka'eleh**
	shnah-yim kah-*eh*-leh
	שניים כאלה

SHOP ASSISTANT

Can I help you?	**Efshar la'azor lekha (m)/lakh (f)?**
	ehf-*shahr* lah-ah-*zor* leh-*khah*/lahkh
	אפשר לעזור לך?
What would you like?	**Mah atah rotseh (m.)/at rotsah?**
	(f.)
	mah ah-*tah* roht-*seh*/aht roht-*sah*
	מה את/ה רוצה?
Will that be all?	**Zeh hakol?**
	zeh hah-*kohl*
	זה הכל?
Would you like anything else?	**Od mashehu?**
	ohd *mah*-sheh-hoo
	עוד משהו?
Would you like it wrapped?	**La'atof et zeh?**
	lah-ah-*tohf* et zeh
	לעטוף את זה?

Sorry, none left	**Mitsta'er, eyn yoter** mits-tah-*ehr*, ehn yoh-*ter* מצטער, אין יותר
I haven't got any	**Eyn li** *ehn* lee אין לי
How many do you want?	**Kamah atah rotseh?** *kah*-mah ah-*tah* roh-*tseh* כמה אתה רוצה?
Is that enough?	**Zeh maspik?** zeh mahs-*pik* זה מספיק?

Shopping for food

Bread

ESSENTIAL INFORMATION

● Bread, like several other basic foodstuffs, is subsidized, and sold at a relatively low price. Two basic kinds, known as 'white bread' (lekhem lah-*vahn*) and 'black bread' (lekhem shah-*khor*), are subsidized. All other kinds are not.

WHAT TO SAY

Some bread, please	**Lekhem bevakashah**
	leh-khem beh-vah-kah-*shah*
	לחם בבקשה
One loaf (like that)	**Kikar akhat (kazot)**
	kee-*kahr* ah-*khaht* (kah-*zot*)
	ככר אחת (כזאת)
Half a loaf	**Khatsi kikar**
	khaht-*si* kee-*kahr*
	חצי ככר
'White' bread	**Lekhem lavan**
	leh-khem lah-*vahn*
	לחם לבן
'Black' bread	**Lekhem shakhor**
	leh-khem shah-*khor*
	לחם שחור
A wholewheat loaf	**Lekhem khita mele'ah**
	leh-khem khee-*tah* meh-leh-*ah*
	לחם חיטה מלאה
A French-style loaf	**Baget**
	bah-*ghet*
	בגט
A loaf of rye bread	**Lekhem khay**
	leh-khem khye
	לחם חי
A bread roll	**Lakhmaniyah**
	lahkh-mah-nee-*yah*
	לחמניה
Some sliced bread	**Lekhem paroos**
	leh-khem pah-*roos*
	לחם פרוס

Two loaves	**Shtey kikarot**
	shtehy kee-kah-*rot*
	שתי ככרות
Four bread rolls	**Arba lakhmaniyot**
	ahr-bah lahkh-mah-nee-*yot*
	ארבע לחמניות

[For other essential expressions see 'Shop talk' p.57]

Cakes, ice cream and sweets

ESSENTIAL INFORMATION

- There are two basic kinds of cakes and pastries in Israel – the 'oriental', predominantly Arab type, and the better known 'western' (European, American) variety. They are usually sold in different places, although some bakeries and cafés provide both.
- There is also a range of salty pastries called 'boorekas'.
- For a selection of cakes and pastries, see list below.

WHAT TO SAY

100 grams of . . .	**Me'ah gram . . .**
	meh-ah grahm
	. . . מאה גרם
200 grams of . . .	**Maatayim gram . . .**
	mah-*tah*-yim grahm
	. . . מאתיים גרם
½ kilo of . . .	**Khatsi kilo . . .**
	khah-*tsi kih*-loh
	. . . חצי קילו
1 kilo of . . .	**Kilo . . .**
	kih-loh
	. . . קילו
1 portion of . . .	**Manah . . .**
	mah-*nah*
	. . . מנה
2 portions of . . .	**Shtey manot . . .**
	shtehy mah-*not*
	. . . שתי מנות

5 portions of . . .   **Khamesh manot . . .**
khah-*mesh* mah-*not*
חמש מנות . . .

    chocolate cake   **oogat shokolad**
ooh-*gaht shoh*-koh-lahd
עוגת שוקולד

    cheese cake   **oogat gvinah**
ooh-*gaht* gvee-*nah*
עוגת גבינה

    apple tart   **oogat tapookhim**
ooh-*gaht* tah-poo-*khim*
עוגת תפוחים

    strawberry pie   **pie toot sadeh**
pye toot sah-*deh*
פאי תות שדה

    baklava   **baklawah**
bahk-*lah*-wah
בקלאווה

    spinach pastry   **boorekas tered**
boo-*reh*-kahs *teh*-red
בורקס תרד

The word for ice-cream is **glidah** (*glee*-dah).

I'd like a(n) . . . ice-cream   **Ani rotseh** (m.)/**rotsah** (f.)
glidat . . .
ah-*nee* rob-*tseh* (m.)/roh-tsah (f.)
glee-*daht* . . .
. . . אני רוצה גלידת

    chocolate   **shokolad**
shoh-koh-lahd
שוקולד

    vanilla   **vanil**
vah-*nil*
וניל

    strawberry   **toot sadeh**
toot sah-*deh*
תות שדה

    apricot   **mishmesh**
mish-*mesh*
משמש

    lemon   **limon**
lee-*mohn*
לימון

peach	**afarsek** ah-fahr-*sek* אפרסק
I'd like a(n) . . . ice-cream	**Ani rotseh (m.)/rotsah (f.)** **glidat . . .** ah-*nee* roh-*tseh* (m.)/roh-tsah (f.) glee-*daht* . . . . . . אני רוצה גלידת
punch-banana	**poonch-bananah** poonch bah-*nah*-nah פונצ' בננה
an ice lolly	**kartiv** *kahr*-tiv קרטיב
a chocolate-coated ice on a stick	**artik metsoopeh shokolad** *ahr*-tik meh-tsoo-*peh* shoh-koh-lahd ארטיק מצופה שוקולד
A packet of . . .	**Khavilat . . .** khah-vee-*laht* . . . חבילת
chocolates	**shokolad** *shoh*-koh-lahd שוקולד
pistachio nuts	**fistookim** fiss-*too*-kim פיסטוקים
A chocolate bar	**Khafisat shokolad** khah-fee-*saht* shoh-koh-lahd חפיסת שוקולד

You may also like to try the following:

oogat pereg ooh-*gaht peh*-reg	a variety of poppyseed cakes and tarts
ozney haman ohz-*nehy* hah-*mahn*	'Haman's ears', a small cake stuffed with poppyseeds or chocolate eaten during the 'Poorim' holiday
soofganiyot soof-gah-nee-*yot*	doughnuts stuffed with jam, eaten during the 'khanookah' holiday
tort egozim tort eh-goh-*zim*	walnut tart
tort shkedim tort shkeh-*dim*	almond tart

'Oriental' sweets:

boormah
boor-mah

baklava in the shape of a turban,
filled with pistachios, steeped in
syrup

kadayef
kah-*tah*-yef

noodle pastry with cream

In the supermarket

ESSENTIAL INFORMATION

- There are several supermarket chains in Israel. Look out for these
  signs:
  SUPERSOL
  CO-OP
  HAMASHBIR
- Hypermarket chains are growing rapidly. They offer a wide range
  of items at low prices. Look out for these signs:
  HYPER-SHOOK
  HYPER-KOL
- For non-food items, see 'Replacing equipment', p.55

WHAT TO SAY

Excuse me, please	**Slikhah** slee-*khah* סליחה
Where is . . .	**Eyfoh . . .** *ehy*-foh איפה . . .
the bread?	**halekhem?** hah-*leh*-khem הלחם?
the butter?	**hakhem'ah?** hah-khem-*ah* החמאה?
the cheese?	**hagvinah?** hah-gvee-*nah* הגבינה?

Where is . . .	**Eyfoh . . .**
	ehy-foh
	. . . איפה
the chocolate?	**hashokolad?**
	hah-*shoh*-koh-lahd
	השוקולד?
the coffee?	**hakafeh?**
	hah-kah-*feh*
	הקפה?
the cooking oil?	**shemen hatigoon?**
	sheh-men hah-tee-*goon*
	שמן הטיגון?
the frozen food?	**hamazon hakafoo?**
	hah-mah-*zon* hah-kah-*foo*
	המזון הקפוא?
the fruit?	**haperot?**
	hah-peh-*roht*
	הפרות?
the (fruit) juices?	**ha-mits?**
	hah-*mits*
	המיץ?
the jam?	**haribah?**
	hah-ree-*bah*
	הריבה?
the meat?	**habasar?**
	hah-bah-*sahr*
	הבשר?
the milk?	**hakhalav?**
	hah-khah-*lahv*
	החלב?
the mineral water?	**hamayim hamineraliyim?**
	hah-*mah*-yim hah-mee-neh-*rah*-lee-yim
	המים המינרליים?
the pasta?	**ha'itriyot?**
	hah-eet-ree-*yot*
	האיטריות?
the salt?	**ha-melakh?**
	hah-*meh*-lahkh
	המלח?
the tea?	**ha-teh?**
	hah-*teh*
	התה?

the tinned fish?	**ha-sardinim?**
	hah-sahr-*dee*-nim
	?הסרדינים
the tinned products?	**koofsa'ot hashimoorim?**
	koof-sah-*oht* hah-shee-moo-*rim*
	?קופסאות השימורים
the vegetables?	**hayerakot?**
	hah-yeh-rah-*kot*
	?הירקות
the vinegar?	**hakhomets?**
	hah-*khoh*-mets
	?החומץ
the wine?	**hayayin?**
	hah-*yah*-yin
	?היין
the yogurt?	**ha-yogoort?**
	hah-*yoh*-goort
	?היוגורט
Where are . . .	**Eyfoh . . .**
	ehy-foh
	. . . איפה
the biscuits?	**habiskvitim?**
	hah-biss-*kvee*-tim
	?הביסקויטים
the crisps?	**hah-khatifim?**
	hah-khah-tee-*fim*
	?החטיפים
the eggs?	**ha-beytsim?**
	hah-behy-*tsim*
	?הביצים
the soft drinks?	**hamashka'ot hakalim?**
	hah-mahsh-kah-*oht* hah-kah-*lim*
	?המשקאות הקלים
the sweets?	**ha-mamtakim?**
	hah-mahm-tah-*kim*
	?הממתקים

[For other essential expressions see 'Shop talk', p.57]

Picnic food

ESSENTIAL INFORMATION

- Many 'delicatessen'-style stores sell picnic food. Most products, however, can be bought at groceries or supermarkets.
- Try 'pitah', a convenient bread for picnics.
- 150g (4–6oz) of prepared salad, if eaten as a starter to a substantial meal.
- 100g (3–4oz) of prepared salad per person, if eaten as the main part of a picnic-type meal.
- Israel is predominantly Jewish and Muslim. Pork products are sold only in 'non-kosher' stores.

WHAT TO SAY

One slice of . . .	**Proosat . . .** proo-*saht* . . . פרוסת
Two slices of . . .	**Shtey proosot . . .** shtehy proo-*soht* . . . שתי פרוסות
roast beef	**rostbif** *rohst*-biff רוסטביף
tongue	**lashon** lah-*shohn* לשון
ham	**shinken** *sheen*-ken שינקן
sausage (salami)	**naknik (salami)** nahk-*nik* (sah-*lah*-mee) נקניק (סלמי)
100 grams of . . .	**Me'ah gram . . .** *meh*-ah grahm . . . מאה גרם
150 grams of . . .	**Me'ah vekhamishim gram . . .** meh-*ah* veh-khah-mee-*shim* grahm . . . מאה וחמישים גרם

200 grams of . . .	**Maatayim gram . . .** mah-*tah*-yim grahm מאתיים גרם . . .
300 grams of . . .	**Shlosh me'ot gram . . .** shlohsh meh-*oht* grahm שלוש מאות גרם . . .
Russian salad	**salat tapukhey adamah** sah-*laht* tah-poo-*khey* ah-dah-*mah* סלט תפוחי אדמה
tomato salad	**salat agvaniyot** sah-*laht* ahg-vah-nee-*yot* סלט עגבניות
beetroot salad	**salat selek** sah-*laht seh*-lek סלט סלק
carrot salad	**salat gezer** sah-*laht gheh*-zehr סלט גזר
green salad	**salat khassah** sah-*laht khah*-sah סלט חסה
cabbage salad	**salat kroov** sah-*laht* kroov סלט כרוב
mixed salad	**salat yerakot** sah-*laht* yeh-rah-*kot* סלט ירקות
mushroom salad	**salat pitriyot** sah-*laht* peet-ree-*yot* סלט פטריות
olives	**zeytim** zehy-*tim* זיתים
anchovies	**anchovi** ahn-*choh*-vee אנצ׳ובי
cheese	**gvinah** gvee-*nah* גבינה
A (pot of) mayonnaise	**(Tsintsenet) mayonez** (tsin-*tseh*-net) mah-yoh-*nez* (צנצנת) מיונז

A (tube of) mustard

(Shfoferet) khardal
(shfoh-*feh*-ret) khahr-*dahl*
שפופרת חרדל

You might also like to try some of these:

khoomus
khoo-moos
חומוס

chickpea salad

tkhinah
tkhee-nah
טחינה

a paste made of sesame seeds,
with lemon and garlic

tabooleh
tah-boo-leh
טבולה

cracked wheat, tomato, parsley,
onion and pepper

labaneh
lah-bah-neh
לבנה

cheese made from sheep's milk,
steeped in olive oil

skhoog
skhoog
סחוג

a spicy yemenite sauce, made with
hot pepper and garlic

Fruit and vegetables

ESSENTIAL INFORMATION

- Israel offers an amazing variety of fruit and vegetables. Since most
  of them are locally grown, prices may vary a great deal according to
  season.
- A kilo is roughly equivalent to 2lbs.

WHAT TO SAY

½ a kilo of . . .

Khatsi kilo . . .
khah-*tsi kee*-loh
. . . חצי קילו

1 kilo of . . .

Kilo . . .
kih-loh
. . . קילו

2 kilos of ...	Shney kilo ... shnehy *kih*-loh שני קילו ...
apples	tapookhim tah-poo-*khim* תפוחים
bananas	bananot bah-*nah*-not בננות
cherries	doovdevanim doov-deh-vah-*nim* דובדבנים
grapes	anavim ah-nah-*vim* ענבים
oranges	tapoozim tah-poo-*zim* תפוזים
pears	agassim ah-gah-*sim* אגסים
peaches	afarsekim ah-fahr-seh-*kim* אפרסקים
plums	shezifim sheh-zee-*fim* שזיפים
strawberries	toot sadeh toot sah-*deh* תות שדה
A pineapple, please	Ananas ekhad bevakashah *ah*-nah-nahs eh-*khahd* beh-vah-kah-*shah* אננס אחד בבקשה
A grapefruit	Eshkolit ehsh-koh-*lit* אשכולית
A melon	Milon mee-*lohn* מילון
A water melon	Avatiyakh ah-vah-*tee*-ahkh אבטיח

1 kilo of . . .	Kilo . . .
	kih-loh
	קילו . . .
artichokes	artishok
	ahr-tee-*shok*
	ארטישוק
aubergines	khatsilim
	khah-tsee-*lim*
	חצילים
carrots	gezer
	gheh-zehr
	גזר
courgettes	kishoo'im
	kee-shoo-*eem*
	קישואים
cucumbers	melafefonim
	meh-lah-feh-foh-*nim*
	מלפפונים
green beans	she'oo'it yerookah
	sheh-ooh-*it* yeh-roo-*kah*
	שעוצית ירוקה
leeks	kreshah
	kreh-*shah*
	כרשה
mushrooms	pitriyot
	pit-ree-*yot*
	פטריות
onions	batsal
	bah-*tsahl*
	בצל
peas	afoonah
	ah-foo-*nah*
	אפונה
potatoes	tapookhey adamah
	tah-poo-*khehy* ah-dah-*mah*
	תפוחי אדמה
pumpkin	dia'at
	dlah-aht
	דלעת
red cabbage	kroov adom
	kroov ah-*dohm*
	כרוב אדום

spinach	**tered**
	teh-red
	תרד
tomatoes	**agvaniyot**
	ahg-vah-nee-*yot*
	עגבניות
A bunch of parsley	**Tsror petroziliya**
	tsrohr peht-roh-*zeel*-yah
	צרור פטרוזיליה
A bunch of radishes	**Tsror tsnoniyot**
	tsrohr tsnoh-nee-*yot*
	צרור צנוניות
A head of garlic	**Rosh shoom**
	rohsh shoom
	ראש שום
A lettuce	**Khasah**
	khah-sah
	חסה
A cauliflower	**Kroovit**
	kroo-*vit*
	כרובית
A cabbage	**Kroov**
	kroov
	כרוב
Like that, please	**Kazeh bevakashah**
	kah-*zeh* beh-vah-kah-*shah*
	כזה בבקשה

Meat

ESSENTIAL INFORMATION

- Weight guide: 125g–200g (4–6oz) of meat per person for one meal.
- A wide range of cuts is available, though you may not find exactly the same ones as at home. If in doubt tell the butcher whether you intend to stew, grill or roast the meat, so that he will know what to give you.
- If you want the best quality mince, choose a piece of meat and ask the butcher to mince it for you.
- Frozen meat can be bought in supermarkets and groceries.
- Most butcher shops are kosher, and do not sell pork or other kinds of non-kosher meat.
  There are numerous laws concerning 'kosher' and 'non kosher' food. These are the main rules that apply to meat:
- Only certain kinds of meat are allowed – beef, lamb, goat, chicken and several other fowl. Other kinds, like pork or game, are forbidden.
- It should be slaughtered in a particular manner, using a special knife.
- Meat or fowl should not be cooked, prepared or served with milk or dairy products. Meat and dairy products cannot be eaten in the same meal. For example, after a meal which includes meat, a kosher restaurant will not serve coffee with milk.

WHAT TO SAY

For a joint, choose the type of meat you want and then say how many people it is for and how you intend to cook it.

Some beef, please	**Bsar bakar bevakashah** bsahr bah-*kahr* beh-vah-kah-*shah* בשר בקר בבקשה
Some lamb	**Bsar taleh** bsahr tah-*leh* בשר טלה
Some mutton	**Bsar keves** bsahr *keh*-vess בשר כבש
Some veal	**Bsar egel** bsahr *eh*-ghel בשר עגל

A joint . . .	**Khatikhat basar**
	khah-tee-*khaht* bah-*sahr*
	חתיכת בשר
Meat for shish kebabs . . .	**Basar le-shishlik** . . .
	bahsahr leh-shish-lik
	. . . בשר לשישליק
for two people	**le-shnayim**
	leh-*shnah*-yim
	לשניים
for four people	**le-shloshah**
	leh-shloh-*shah*
	לשלושה
for six people	**le-shishah**
	leh-shee-*shah*
	לשישה
I want . . . the meat	**Ani rotseh** (m.)/**rotsah** (f.). . .
	et habasar
	ah-*nee* roh-*tseh* (m.)
	/roh-*tsah* (f.). . . eht hah-bah-*sahr*
	אני רוצה . . . את הבשר
to boil	**levashel**
	leh-vah-*shel*
	לבשל
to grill	**litslot**
	lits-*loht*
	לצלות
to roast	**le'efot**
	leh-eh-*foht*
	לאפות

For steak, liver and kidneys, do as above.

Some steak, please	**Steyk bevakashah**
	stehyk beh-vah-kah-*shah*
	סטייק בבקשה
Some liver	**Kaved**
	kah-*vehd*
	כבד
Some kidneys . . .	**Klayot** . . .
	klah-*yot*
	. . . כליות
for three people	**le-shloshah**
	leh-shloh-*shah*
	לשלושה

for five people	**le-khamishah**
	leh-khah-mee-*shah*
	לחמישה

For chops, do it this way:

Two veal escalopes, please	**Shtey proosot bsar egel,**
	bevakashah
	shtehy proo-*soht* bsahr *eh*-ghel,
	beh-vah-kah-*shah*
	שתי פרוסות בשר עגל, בבקשה

Five lamp chops	**Khamesh tsla'ot taleh**
	khah-*mesh* tslah-*oht* tah-*leh*
	חמש צלעות טלה

Beef and veal
Bahkahr veh-ehghel בקר ועגל

1 tsah-*vahr*	צואר
2 kah-*tehf*	כתף
3 zroh-ah	זרוע
4 khah-*zeh*	חזה
5 tslah-*oht*	צלעות
6 moh-ten	מותן
7 fee-*leh*	פילה
8 rohsh yeh-reh-*khah*	ידבה
	ראש
9 Yeh-reh-*khah*	ירכה
10 shohk	שוק

Lamb and mutton
tah*leh* veh-*keh*-vess טלה וכבש

1 tsah-*vahr*	צואר
2 shohk	שוק
3 tslah-*oht*	צלעות
4 fee-*leh*	פילה
5 khah-*zeh*	חזה
6 yah-*rekh*	ירך

You may also want:

A chicken	**Off**
	ohf
	עוף

A duck	**Barvaz**
	bahr-*vahz*
	ברוז

A turkey	**Hodoo**
	hoh-doo
	הודו
A dove	**Yonah**
	yoh-*nah*
	יונה
A rabbit	**Arnav**
	ahr-*nahv*
	ארנב
Some tongue	**Lashon**
	lah-*shohn*
	לשון
Some (chicken) hearts	**Levavot off**
	leh-vah-*voht* (ohf)
	לבבות (עוף)

[Other essential expressions see also 'Shop talk', p.57]

Please . . .	**Bevakashah . . .**
	beh-vah-kah-*shah*
	. . . בבקשה
mince it	**titkhan** (m.)/**titkhani** (f.) **et zeh**
	tit-*khahn* (m.)/tit-khah-nee (f.) eht ze
	תטחן/תטחני את זה
dice it	**takhtokh** (m.)/**takhtekhi** (f.) **le-koobiyot**
	tahkh-*tokh* (m.)/tahkh-teh-*khee* (f.) leh-koo-bee-*yot*
	תחתוך/תחתכי לקוביות
trim the fat	**torid** (m.)/**toridi** (f.) **et hashooman**
	toh-*rid* (m.)/toh-*ree*-dee (f.) eht hah-shoo-*mahn*
	תוריד/י את השומן

Fish

ESSENTIAL INFORMATION

- Weight guide: 250g (8oz) minimum per person for one meal of fish
  bought on the bone.

  i.e. ½ kilo/500g   for two people

      1 kilo   for four people

      1½ kilo   for six people
- Some fish are better known by their Arab name, while others have
  Hebrew names. When both names are used, the lesser known is
  given in brackets.

WHAT TO SAY

Fish is bought by the kilo, or by the item. When the fish are small, the
fishmonger will offer an approximation of the weight required.

[For numbers see p.135]

½ a kilo of . . .	**Khatsi kilo . . .**
	khah-*tsi kee*-loh
	חצי קילו . . .
1 kilo of . . .	**Kilo . . .**
	kih-loh
	קילו . . .
1½ kilos of . . .	**Kilo vakhetsi . . .**
	kih-loh vah-*kheh*-tsi
	קילו וחצי . . .
One . . .	**. . . ekhad**
	eh-*khahd*
	אחד . . .
Two . . .	**Shney . . .**
	shnehy
	שני . . .
Three . . .	**Shloshah . . .**
	shloh-*shah*
	שלושה . . .
carp	**karpiyon**
	kahr-pee-*yon*
	קרפיון

cod	**bakalah**	
	bah-kah-lah	
	בקלה	
Jaffa cod	**lokoos (dakar)**	
	loh-koos (dah-*kahr*)	
	לוקוס	
lobster	**lobster (sartan)**	
	lobster (sahr-*tahn*)	
	(לובסטר (סרטן	
nile princess	**nessikhat ha-niloos**	
	neh-see-*khaht* hah-*nee*-loos	
	נסיכת הנילוס	
red mullet (small)	**barboonyas**	
	bahr-*boon*-yas	
	ברבוניים	
salmon	**salmon**	
	sahl-mon	
	סלמון	
sardine	**sardin**	
	sahr-*din*	
	סרדין	
shrimps	**shrimps**	
	shrimps	
	שרימפס	
sole	**sol**	
	sohl	
	סול	
squid	**kalamari**	
	kah-lah-*mah*-ri	
	קלמרי	
St Peter's fish	**moosht (amnoon)**	
	moosht (ahm-*noon*)	
	(מושט (אמנון	
striped mullet	**boori**	
	boo-ree	
	בורי	
trout	**forel**	
	foh-*rel*	
	פורל	

Some large fish can be purchased by the slice:

One slice of . . .	Proosat . . .
	proo-*saht*
	פרוסת . . .
Two slices of . . .	Shtey proosot . . .
	shtehy proo-*sot*
	שתי פרוסות . . .
Three slices of . . .	Shalosh proosot . . .
	shah-*losh* proo-*sot*
	שלוש פרוסות . . .
cod	bakalah
	bah-kah-lah
	בקלה
Jaffa cod	lokoos
	loh-koos
	לוקוס
tuna	toonah
	too-nah
	טונה

Shellfish

Crab	Sartan
	sahr-*tahn*
	סרטן
Oysters	Tsdafot
	tsdah-*fot*
	צדפות
Shrimps	Shrimps
	shrimps
	שרימפס

[Other essential expressions see also 'Shop talk', p.57]

Please	Bevakashah . . .
	beh-vah-kah-*shah*
	בבקשה . . .
take the head off	torid et harosh
	toh-*rid* eht hah-*rohsh*
	תוריד את הראש
clean them	tenakeh otam
	teh-nah-*keh* oh-*tahm*
	תנקה אותם

Eating and Drinking out

Ordering a drink

ESSENTIAL INFORMATION

- Pubs and bars have become very popular and can be found almost everywhere.
- Except in places where drinks are consumed standing at a counter, there is nearly always waiter service and one should leave a tip of 10–15 per cent.
- The quality of local wines is improving, and some kinds are excellent. On the other hand, ever since Israelis have discovered wine, prices are rising.
- Good quality local beer is sold in cans or bottles. Bars and pubs serve draught lager.
- There are no licensing laws and children are allowed in.

WHAT TO SAY

I'd like . . .	**Ani rotseh** (m.)/**rotsah** (f.) . . . ah-*nee* roh-*tseh* (m.)/roh-tsah (f.) אני רוצה . . .
a black coffee	**kafeh shakhor** kah-*feh* shah-*khor* קפה שחור
a filter coffee	**kafeh filter** kah-*feh* fil-ter קפה פילטר
a Nescafé	**neskafeh** *ness*-kah-feh נס קפה
a Turkish coffee	**kafeh toorki** kah-*feh* toor-*kee* קפה טורקי
a hot chocolate/a tea	**shoko kham/teh** *shoh*-koh khahm/teh תה/שוקו חם
without sugar	**bli sookar** blee soo-*kahr* בלי סוכר

I'd like . . .	**Ani rotseh (m.)/rotsah (f.)** . . .
	ah-*nee* roh-*tseh* (m.)/roh-tsah (f.)
	. . . אני רוצה
with a little sugar	**im me'at sookar**
	eem meh-*aht* soo-*kahr*
	עם מעט סוכר
sweet	**matok**
	mah-*tok*
	מתוק
with milk	**im khalav**
	eem khah-*lahv*
	עם חלב
with lemon	**im limon**
	eem lee-*mon*
	עם לימון
a glass of milk	**kos khalav**
	koss khah-*lahv*
	כוס חלב
two glasses of milk	**shtey kossot khalav**
	shtehy koh-*sot* khah-*lahv*
	שתי כוסות חלב
a bottle of . . .	**bakbook** . . .
	bahk-*book*
	בקבוק . . .
a can of . . .	**pakhit** . . .
	pah-*khit*
	. . . פחית
mineral water	**mayim mineraliyim**
	mah-yim mee-neh-*rah*-lee-yim
	מים מינרליים
a lemonade	**limonada**
	lee-moh-*nah*-dah
	לימונדה
a lemon juice	**mits limon**
	meets lee-*mohn*
	מיץ לימון
an orange juice (natural)	**mits tapoozim (tiv'l)**
	meets tah-poo-*zim* (teev-*ee*)
	מיץ תפוזים (טבעי)
a grape juice	**mits anavim**
	mits ah-nah-*veem*
	מיץ ענבים

a grapefruit juice	**mits eshkoliyot**
	meets ehsh-koh-lee-*yot*
	מיץ אשכוליות
an apple juice	**mits tapookhim**
	meets tah-poo-*khim*
	מיץ תפוחים
a Coca-Cola	**kolah**
	koh-lah
	קולה
a bottle of beer	**bakbook birah**
	bahk-*book bee*-rah
	בקבוק בירה
a can of beer	**pakhit birah**
	pah-*kheet bee*-rah
	פחית בירה
a draught beer	**birah mehakhavit**
	bee-rah meh-hah-khah-*vit*
	בירה מהחבית
small	**ktanah**
	ktah-*nah*
	קטנה
large	**gdolah**
	gdoh-*lah*
	גדולה
a bottle of wine	**bakbook yayin**
	bahk-*book yah*-yin
	בקבוק יין
a small bottle of wine	**bakbook yayin katan**
	bahk-*book yah*-yin kah-*tahn*
	בקבוק יין קטן
red	**adom**
	ah-*dom*
	אדום
white	**lavan**
	lah-*vahn*
	לבן
rosé	**rozeh**
	roh-*zeh*
	רוזה
dry	**yavesh**
	yah-*vesh*
	יבש

I'd like . . .	**Ani rotseh (m.)/rotsah (f.) . . .**
	ah-*nee* roh-*tseh* (m.)/roh-tsah (f.)
	. . . אני רוצה
medium sweet	**khatsi yavesh**
	khaht-*see* yah-*vesh*
	חצי יבש
sparkling	**tossess**
	toh-*sess*
	תוסס
a bottle of champagne	**bakbook shampanyah**
	bahk-*book shahm*-pahn-yah
	בקבוק שמפניה
a whisky	**wiski**
	wiss-kee
	ויסקי
with ice	**im kerakh**
	eem *keh*-rahkh
	עם קרח
with water	**im mayim**
	eem *mah*-yim
	עם מים
with soda	**im sodah**
	eem *soh*-dah
	עם סודה
a gin	**jin**
	jin
	ג'ין
a gin and tonic	**jin and tonic**
	jin and tonic
	ג'ין אנד טוניק
with lemon	**im limon**
	eem lee-*mon*
	עם לימון
a vodka	**vodkah**
	vohd-kah
	וודקה
a vodka and tonic	**vodka and tonic**
	vodka and tonic
	וודקה אנד טוניק
a brandy/cognac	**konyak**
	kohn-yahk
	קוניאק

Other essential expressions:

Waiter! Waitress!	**Meltsar!** (m.)/**meltsarit!** (f.) mehl-*tsahr* (m.)/mehl-tsah-*rit* (f.) מלצר!/מלצרית!
Excuse me	**Slikhah** slee-*khah* סליחה
The bill, please	**Hakheshbon bevakashah** hah-khesh-*bohn* beh-vah-kah-*shah* החשבון בבקשה
How much?	**Kamah zeh?** *kah*-mah zeh כמה זה?
Is service included?	**Zeh kolel sheroot?** zeh koh-*lel* sheh-*root* זה כולל שרות?
Where is the toilet please?	**Slikhah, eyfoh hasherootim?** slee-*khah, ehy*-foh hah-sheh-*root*-*tim* סליחה, איפה השרותים?

Ordering a snack

ESSENTIAL INFORMATION

- Most coffee houses offer a variety of savoury snacks.
- There are cafeterias specializing in salty, 'boorekas' style dishes (see below).
- For picnic type snacks see p.70.

WHAT TO SAY

I'd like . . .	**Ani rotseh** (m.)/**rotsah** (f.) . . . ah-*nee* roh-*tseh* (m.)/roh-tsah (f.) . . . אני רוצה
a cheese roll	**lakhmaniyah im gvinah** lahkh-mah-nee-*yah* eem gvee-*nah* לחמניה עם גבינה

I'd like . . .	**Ani rotseh (m.)/rotsah (f.)** . . .
	ah-*nee* roh-*tseh* (m.)/roh-tsah (f.)
	. . . אני רוצה
an egg roll	**lakhmaniyah im beytsah**
	lahkh-mah-nee-*yah* eem behy-*tsah*
	לחמניה עם ביצה
a hamburger	**hamburger**
	hahm-boor-gher
	המבורגר
a hot dog	**naknikiyah be-lakhmaniya**
	nahk-nee-kee-*yah* beh-lahk-mah-nee-*yah*
	נקניקיה בלחמניה
a toasted sandwich	**tost**
	tohst
	טוסט
an ice-cream	**glidah**
	glee-dah
	גלידה
a bag of crisps	**sakit chips**
	sah-*kit* chips
	שקית צ׳יפס

You may also like to try the following:

falafel	balls of ground chickpeas and
fah-*lah*-fel	spices, fried in oil, served in pitah.
פלאפל	
shawarmah	sheep or turkey meat roasted on a
shah-*wahr*-mah	spit, in pitah
שוארמה	
khoomoos	chickpea salad, served in pitah or
khoo-moos	on a plate
חומוס	
boorekas	savoury pastries filled with cheese,
boo-*reh*-kahs	spinach, minced meat, etc.
בורקס	

In a restaurant

ESSENTIAL INFORMATION

- The place to ask for: **miss'adah** (miss-ah-*dah*).
- By law menus and prices must be displayed in the restaurant.
- It is important to check whether the service charge is included in the bill. If it isn't, a tip of 10–15 per cent is customary. If service charge is included, a further small tip is usually left if one is pleased with the service.
- Most restaurants are open to 11 or 12 midnight.
- Children's portions are usually available.
- Kosher restaurants will not serve pork, and if meat dishes are included in the menu, no dairy products will be served.

WHAT TO SAY

May I book a table?	**Efshar lehazmin shoolkhan?**
	ehf-*shahr* leh-hahz-min shool-*khahn*
	אפשר להזמין שולחן?
I've booked a table	**Hizmanti shoolkhan**
	heez-*mahn*-ti shool-*khahn*
	הזמנתי שולחן
A table ...	**Shoolkhan ...**
	shool-*khahn*
	... שולחן
for one	**le'ekhad**
	leh-eh-*khahd*
	לאחד
for thee	**le-shloshah**
	leh-shloh-*shah*
	לשלושה
The menu, please	**Et ha-tafrit bevakashah**
	eht hah-tahf-*rit* beh-vah-kah-*shah*
	את התפריט בבקשה
Today's special menu	**Et hatafrit shel hayom**
	eht hah-tahf-*rit* shel hah-*yom*
	את התפריט של היום
What's this please?	**Slikhah, mah zeh?**
	slee-*khah*, mah zeh
	סליחה, מה זהז

Some wine, please	**Yayin bevakashah** *yah*-yin beh-vah-kah-*shah* יין בבקשה
A bottle	**Bakbook** bahk-*book* בקבוק
A half bottle	**Khatsi bakbook** khaht-*si* bahk-*book* חצי בקבוק
Red/white/rosé	**Adom/lavan/rozeh** ah-*dom*/lah-*vahn*/roh-*zeh* אדום/לבן/רוזה
Some beer	**Birah** *bee*-rah בירה
Some more bread, please	**Od lekhem bevakashah** ohd *leh*-khem beh-vah-kah-*shah* עוד לחם בבקשה
Some more wine	**Od yayin** ohd *yah*-yin עוד יין
Some oil	**Shemen** *sheh*-men שמן
Some vinegar	**Khomets** *khoh*-mets חומץ
Some salt	**Melakh** *meh*-lahkh מלח
Some pepper	**Pilpel** *pill*-pel פלפל
Some mineral water	**Mayim minerallyim** *mah*-yim mee-neh-*rah*-lee-yim מים מינרליים
How much does that come to?	**Kamah zeh sakh hakol?** *kah*-mah zeh sahkh hah-*kol* כמה זה סך הכל?
Is service included?	**Zeh kolel sheroot?** zeh koh-*lel* sheh-*root* זה כולל שרות?

Where is the toilet, please?	**Slikhah, eyfoh hasherootim?**
	slee-*khah*, *ehy*-foh hah-sheh-roo-*tim*
	סליחה, איפה השרותים?
Excuse me! *[when trying to get the waiter's attention]*	**Slikhah!**
	slee-*khah*
	סליחה!
The bill, please	**Hakheshbon bevakashah**
	hah-khesh-*bohn* beh-vah-kah-*shah*
	החשבון בבקשה
May I have a receipt	**Efshar lekabel kabala?**
	ehf-*shahr* leh-kah-*bel* kah-bah-*lah*
	אפשר לקבל קבלה?

Key words for courses as seen on some menus

[Only ask this question if you want the waiter to remind you of the choice]

What have you got in the way of . . .	**Eyzeh . . . yesh lakhem?**
	ehy-zeh . . . yesh lah-*khem*
	איזה . . . יש לכם?
starters?	**manot rishonot**
	mah-*not* ree-shoh-*not*
	מנות ראשונות
soup?	**marakim**
	mah-rah-*kim*
	מרקים
egg dishes?	**ma'akhaley beytsim**
	mah-ah-kha-*lehy* behy-*tsim*
	מאכלי ביצים
fish?	**soogey dagim**
	soo-*ghehy* dah-*ghim*
	סוגי דגים
meat?	**soogey basar**
	soo-*ghehy* bah-*sahr*
	סוגי בשר
main dishes?	**manot ikariyot**
	mah-*not* ee-kah-ree-*yot*
	מנות עיקריות
grills?	**soogey gril**
	soo-*ghehy* grill
	סוגי גריל

What have you got in the way of . . .	Eyzeh . . . yesh lakhem? *ehy*-zeh . . . yesh lah-*khem* איזה . . . יש לכם?
vegetables?	yerakot yeh-rah-*kot* ירקות
salads?	salatim sah-*lah*-tim סלטים
cheese?	gvinot gvee-*not* גבינות
fruit?	perot peh-*rot* פרות
ice-cream?	glidot *glee*-dot גלידות
desserts?	kinuakh kee-*noo*-ahkh קינוח

UNDERSTANDING THE MENU

- Most menus have an English translation, although some words may be incomprehensible.
- In some oriental-style restaurants it is the custom to bring a large tray of starters to the table, from which you can choose the ones you want.
- You will find the names of the principal ingredients of most dishes on these pages:

Starters, see p.70	Fruit, see p.72
Meat, see p.76	Dessert, see p.64
Fish, see p.80	Cheese, see p.67
Vegetables, see p.72	Ice-cream, see p.65

- If no translation exists, the following list of cooking and menu terms should help you to understand the offered choice:

ah-dah-*shim* עדשים	lentils
ahg-vah-nee-*yot* עגבניות	tomatoes
ah-*lehy gheh*-fen עלי גפן	(stuffed) vine leaves

bah-*kahr* בקר	beef
bah-*sahr* בשר	meat
bah-tah-*noor* בתנור	baked or roasted in the oven
bah-*tsahl* בצל	onion
beh-*roh*-tev ברוטב	with sauce
behy-*tsah* ביצה	egg
(behy-*tsah*) ah-yin ביצת עין	fried egg
behy-*tsah* rah-*kah* ביצה רכה	soft-boiled egg
behy-*tsash* kah-*shah* ביצה קשה	hard-boiled egg
boo-*reh*-kahs בורקס	savoury pastry filled with cheese, spinach, etc.
dahg דג	fish
dahg mah-*loo*-ahkh דג מלוח	pickled fish
gheh-zer גזר	carrots
gvee-*nah* גבינה	cheese
gvee-*nah* leh-vah-*nah* גבינה לבנה	'white' (cream) cheese
gvee-*nah* tseh-hoo-*bah* גבינה צהובה	'yellow' cheese (all kinds)
kah-*bahb* קבב	kebab
kah-*ved* כבד	liver
kahr קר	cold
kee-shoo-*eem* קישואים	courgettes
keh-vess כבש	mutton
keh-vess bah-tah-*noor* כבש בתנור	roast lamb

khahm חם	hot
khah-*meen* חמין	A stew of beans, potatoes and meat, cooked for a very long time
khah-moo-*tsim* חמוצים	pickled vegetables
khah-sah חסה	lettuce
khah-*tsil* חציל	aubergine
khah-vee-*tah* חביתה	omelette
khem-*aah* חמאה	butter
klah-*yot* כליות	kidneys
kroov כרוב	cabbage
kroo-*vit* כרובית	cauliflower
ktsee-*tsot* קציצות	meatballs
lahkh-mah-nee-*yah* לחמניה	bread roll
leh-khem לחם	bread
lee-*mon* לימון	lemon
off עוף	chicken
off tsah-*looy* עוף צלוי	grilled chicken
mah-*rahk* מרק	soup
mah-*rahk* hah-*yom* מרק היום	soup of the day
mah-*rahk* off מרק עוף	chicken soup
mah-*rahk* yeh-rah-*kot* מרק ירקות	vegetable soup
mah-yim מים	water
mah-yim mih-neh-*rah-lee*-yim מים מינרליים	mineral water

meh-lah-feh-*fon* מלפפון	cucumber
meh-lahkh מלח	salt
meh-moo-*lah* ממולא	stuffed
meh-voo-*shahl* מבושל	boiled, cooked
nahk-*nik* נקניק	sausage
pill-pel פלפל	pepper
pill-pel meh-moo-*lah* פלפל ממולא	stuffed pepper
peet-ree-*yot* פטריות	mushrooms
pet-roh-*zeel*-yah פטרוזיליה	parsley
nah נא	rare*
sah-*laht* hah-oh-*nah* סלט העונה	salad of the season
sah-*laht* yeh-rah-*kot* סלט ירקות	mixed vegetable salad
seh-lek סלק	beetroot
shee-*pood* שיפוד	spit, shishkebab
sheh-oo-*it* שעועית	beans
shoom שום	garlic
tah-*leh* טלה	lamb
tah-poo-*khehy* ah-dah-*mah* תפוחי אדמה	potatoes
tah-poo-*khim* תפוחים	apples
teh-red תרד	spinach
tslah-*ot* צלעות	spare-ribs

*For broiled or grilled meat use English terms –
well done, medium, medium rare, etc.

tslee **צלי**	roast
zehy-*tim* זיתים	olives
zehy-*tim* shkhoh-*rim* זיתים שחורים	black olives

Health

ESSENTIAL INFORMATION

- In Israel there are both State and privately run medical services. Local inhabitants join one of several medical insurance programmes (**koopat kholim**).
- When you visit Israel it is essential to have proper medical insurance. A policy can be bought through a travel agent, a broker or a motoring organization.
- Take your own personal 'first line' first aid kit with you.
- For minor disorders and treatment at a chemist's, see p.40.
- For finding your way to a doctor, dentist and chemist, see pp.13 and 14
- Once in Israel, decide on a definite plan of action in case of serious illness: explain your problem to a near neighbour, the receptionist or someone you see regularly. You are then dependent on that person helping you to obtain treatment.
- Look for the doctor you need in the Yellow Pages directories. These will have English appendices.
- There are also **Red Magen David** stations (the local equivalent of the Red Cross). Get to the nearest station in case of emergency, or dial 101 for an ambulance service.

WHAT'S THE MATTER

I have a pain . . .	**Ko'ev li . . .** koh-*ev* li . . . כואב לי
in my abdomen	**ba-beten** bah-*beh*-ten בבטן

in my ankle	**ba-karsol**
	bah-kahr-*sol*
	בקרסול
in my arm	**ba-zro'ah**
	bah-*zroh*-ah
	בזרוע
in my back	**ba-gav**
	bah-*gahv*
	בגב
in my bladder	**be-shalpookhit ha-sheten**
	beh-shahl-poo-*khit* hah-*sheh*-ten
	בשלפוחית השתן
in my bowels	**ba-me'ayim**
	bah-meh-*ah*-yim
	במעיים
in my breast	**ba-shad**
	bah-shahd
	בשד
in my chest	**ba-khazeh**
	bah-khah-*zeh*
	בחזה
in my ear	**ba-ozen**
	bah-*oh*-zen
	באחן
in my eye	**ba-ayin**
	bah-*eye*-in
	בעין
in my foot	**be-khaf ha-regel**
	beh-*khaf* hah-*reh*-ghel
	בכף הרגל
in my head	**ba-rosh**
	bah-*rohsh*
	בראש
in my heel	**ba-akev**
	bah-ah-*kev*
	בעקב
in my jaw	**ba-lesset**
	bah-*leh*-set
	בלסת
in my kidneys	**ba-klayot**
	bah-klah-*yot*
	בכליות

I have a pain . . .	**Ko'ev li . . .**
	koh-*ev* li
	כואב לי . . .
in my leg	**ba-regel**
	bah-*reh*-ghel
	ברגל
in my lungs	**ba-re'ot**
	bah-reh-*ot*
	בריאות
in my neck	**ba-tsavar**
	bah-tsah-*vahr*
	בצוואר
in my penis	**ba-pin**
	bah-*pin*
	בפין
in my shoulder	**ba-katef**
	bah-kah-*tef*
	בכתף
in my stomach	**ba-keva**
	bah-keh-*vah*
	בקיבה
in my testicles	**ba-ashakhim**
	bah-ah-shah-*khim*
	באשכים
in my throat	**ba-garon**
	bah-gah-*ron*
	בגרון
in my vagina	**ba-vagina**
	bah-*vah*-ghee-nah
	בווגינה
in my wrist	**be-perek hayad**
	beh-*peh*-rek hah-*yahd*
	בפרק היד
I have a pain here *[point]*	**Ko'ev li kan**
	koh-*ehv* lee kahn
	כואב לי כאן
I have a toothache	**Yesh li ke'ev shinayim**
	yesh lee keh-*ehv* shee-*nah*-yim
	יש לי כאב שיניים
I have broken . . .	**Shavarti et . . .**
	shah-*vahr*-ti eht
	שברתי את . . .

my dentures	**et ha-shinayim hatotavot**
	eht hah-shee-nah-*yim* hah-toh-tah-*vot*
	א השיניים התותבות
my glasses	**et ha-mishkafayim**
	eht hah-mish-kah-*fah*-yim
	א המשקפיים
I have lost my contact lens	**'ibadti adashat maga**
	ee-*bahd*-ti ah-dah-*shaht* mah-*gah*
	איבדתי עדשת מגע
I have lost a filling	**Naflah li stimah**
	nahf-*lah* lee stee-*mah*
	נפלה לי סתימה
My child is ill	**Ha-yeled sheli kholeh** (m)/
	Ha-yaldah sheli kholah (f)
	hah-*yeh*-led sheh-*li* khoh-*leh* (m.)
	hah-yahl-*dah* sheh-*li* khoh-*lah* (f.)
	הילד/ה שלי חולה
He/she has a pain here *[point]*	**Ko'ev lo/lah kan**
[For parts of the body,	koh-*ehv* loh/lah kahn
see list above]	כואב לו/לה כאן
How bad is it?	
I'm ill	**Ani kholeh** (m.)/**kholah** (f.)
	ah-*nee* khoh-*leh* (m.)/khoh-*lah*
	אני חולה
It's urgent	**Zeh dakhoof**
	zeh dah-*khoof*
	זה דחוף
It's serious	**Zeh retsini**
	zeh reh-tsee-*nee*
	זה רציני
It's not serious	**Zeh lo retsini**
	zeh loh reh-tsee-*nee*
	זה לא רציני
It hurts	**Zeh ko'ev**
	zeh koh-*ehv*
	זה כואב
It hurts a lot	**Zeh ko'ev me'od**
	zeh koh-*ehv* meh-*od*
	זה כואב מאוד
It doesn't hurt much	**Zeh lo kol kakh ko'ev**
	zeh loh kohl kahkh koh-*ehv*
	זה לא כל כך כואב

The pain occurs . . .	**Ha-ke'ev mofi'a . . .** hah-keh-*ehv* moh-*fee*-ah . . . הכאב מופיע
every quarter of an hour	**kol reva sha'ah** kol *reh*-vah shah-*ah* כל רבע שעה
every half hour	**kol khahtsi sha'ah** kol khah-*tsi* shah-*ah* כל חצי שעה
every hour	**kol sha'ah** kol shah-*ah* כל שעה
every day	**kol yom** kol yom כל יום
most of the time	**rov hazman** rov hah-*zmahn* רוב הזמן
I've had it for . . .	**Ani margish (m.)/** **margishah (f.) et zeh kvar . . .** ah-*nee* mahr-*ghish* (m.)/ mahr-ghee-*shah* (f.) eht zeh kvahr . . . אני מרגיש/ה את זה כבר
one day/one hour	**sha'ah/yom** shah-*ah*/yom שעה/יום
two hours/two days	**sha'atayim/yomayim** shah-ah-*tah*-yim/yoh-*mah*-yim שעתיים/יומיים
three hours/three days	**shalosh sha'ot/shloshah yamim** shah-*losh* shah-*ot*/shloh-*shah* yah-*mim* שלוש שעות/ שלושה ימים
It's a sharp pain	**Zeh ke'ev khad** zeh keh-*ehv* khahd זה כאב חד
It's a dull pain	**Zeh ke'ev amoom** zeh keh-*ehv* ah-*moom* זה כאב עמום
It's a nagging pain	**Zeh ke'ev matrid** zeh keh-*ehv* maht-*rid* זה כאב מטריד

I feel weak	**Ani margish (m.)/margishah (f.) khoolshah** ah-*nee* mahr-*ghish* (m.)/mahr-ghee-*shah* (f.) khool-*shah* אני מרגיש/ה חולשה
I have a fever	**Yesh li khom** yesh lee khom יש לי חום
I feel dizzy	**Ani margish (m.)/margishah (f.) skharkhoret** ah-*nee* mahr-*gheesh* (m.)/mahr-ghee-*shah* (f.) skhahr-*khoh*-ret אני מרגיש/ה סחרחורת
I feel sick	**Ani margish (m.)/margishah (f.) bkhilah** ah-*nee* mahr-*gheesh* (m.)/mahr-ghee-*shah* (f.) bkhee-*lah* אני מרגיש/ה בחילה

Already under treatment for something else?

I take . . . regularly	**Ani lokeakh (m.)/lokakhat (f.) . . . bekvi'oot** ah-*nee* loh-*keh*-ahkh (m.)/loh-kah-khaht (f.) . . . be-kvee-*oot* אני לוקח/ת . . . בקביעות
this medicine	**et hatroofah hazot** eht hah-troo-*fah* hah-*zot* את התרופה הזאת
these pills	**et hakadoorim ha-eleh** eht hah-kah-doo-*rim* hah-*eh*-leh את הכדורים האלה
I have a heart condition	**Ani kholeh (m.)/kholat (f.) lev** ah-*nee* khoh-*leh* (m.)/khoh-laht (f.) lev אני חולה/חולת לב
I have haemorrhoids	**Yesh li tkhorim** yesh lee tkhoh-*rim* יש לי טחורים
I have rheumatism	**Yesh li romatizm** yesh lee roh-mah-*tee*-zm יש לי רומטיזם
I have diabetes	**Yesh li sookeret** yesh lee soo-*keh*-ret יש לי סוכרת

I have asthma	**Yesh li astmah** yesh lee *ahst*-mah יש לי אסטמה
I am pregnant	**Ani be-herayon** ah-*nee* be-heh-rah-*yon* אני בהריון
I'm allergic to (penicillin)	**Ani alergi (m.)/alergit (f.) le-(penitsilin)** ah-*nee* ah-*ler*-ghi (m.)/ ah-*ler*-gheet (f.) leh-(peh-nee-tsi-*lin*) אני אלרגי ל(פביציליו)

Other essential expressions

Please, can you help?	**Tookhal (m)/tookhli (f) la'azor bevakashah?** too-*khahl*/too-*khlee* lah-ah-*zor* beh-vah-kah-*shah* תוכל/י לעזור בבקשה?
A doctor please	**Rofeh bevakashah** roh-*feh* beh-vah-kah-*shah* רופא בבקשה
A dentist	**Rofeh shinayim** roh-*feh* shee-*nah*-yim רופא שיניים
I don't speak Hebrew	**Ani lo medaber (m.)/medaberet (f.) Ivrit** ah-*nee* loh meh-dah-*ber* (m.)/ meh-dah-beh-ret (f.) ihv-rit אני לא מדבר עברית
What times does . . . arrive?	**Be-eyzeh sha'ah magi'a . . .** beh-*ehy*-zeh shah-*ah* mah-*ghee*-ah באיזה שעה מגיע . . .
the doctor	**ha-rofeh?** hah-roh-*feh* הרופא?
the dentist	**rofeh hashinayim?** roh-*feh* hah-shee-*nah*-yim רופא השיניים

From the doctor: key sentences to understand

Take this . . .	Kakh (m.)/kkhi (f.) et zeh . . .
	kahkh (m.)/k-khee (f.) eht zeh . . .
	קח/י את זה . . .
every day/every hour	kol yom/kol sha'ah
	kol yom/ kol shah-*ah*
	כל יום/כל שעה
(three/four) times a day	(shalosh/arbah) pe'amim be-yom
	(shah-*losh*/*ahr*-bah) peh-ah-*mim* beh-*yom*
	(שלוש/ארבע) פעמים ביום
Stay in bed	Tisha'er (m.)/tisha'ari (f.) ba-mitah
	tee-shah-*ehr* (m.)/ tee-shah-ah-*ree* (f.) bah-mee-*tah*
	תשאר/י במטה
Don't travel . . . for two days/weeks	al tisah (m.)/tisi (f.) (yomayim/shvoo'ayim)
	ahl tee-*sah* (m.)/tiss-*ee* (f.) (yoh-*mah*-yim/shvoo-*ah*-yim)
	אל תיסע/י (יומים/שבועיים)
You must go to hospital	Atah khayav (m.) at khayevet (f.) la-lekhet le-beyt kholim
	ah-*tah* khah-*yahv*/aht khah-*yeh*-vet la-*leh*-khet le-*behyt* khoh-*lim*
	אתה/ה חייב/ת ללכת לבית חולים

Problems: complaints, loss, theft

ESSENTIAL INFORMATION

- The post office, bus companies, taxi companies, etc., have 'lost and found' departments.
- If the worse comes to the worst, find the police station. To ask the way, see p.12.
- If you lose your passport go to the Consulate.
- In an emergency dial 100 for the police, 102 for the fire brigade.

COMPLAINTS

I bought this . . .	**Kaniti et zeh . . .** kah-*nee*-ti eht zeh . . . קניתי את זה
today	**hayom** hah-*yom* היום
yesterday	**etmol** eht-*mol* אתמול
on Monday *[For days of the week see p.142]*	**be-yom sheni** beh-*yom* sheh-*ni* ביום שני
It's no good	**Zeh lo tov** zeh loh tov זה לא טוב
Look	**Tir'eh** teer-*eh* תראה
Here *[point]*	**Hineh** *hee*-neh הנה
Can you change it?	**Tookhal lehakhalif et zeh?** too-*khahl* leh-ha-khah-*lif* eht zeh תוכל להחליף את זה?
Here is the receipt	**Hineh ha-kabalah** *hee*-neh hah-kah-bah-*lah* הנה הקבלה

Can I have a refund?	Tookhloo le-hakhazir li et ha-kessef? tookh-*loo* leh-hah-khah-*zir* lee eht hah-*keh*-sef תוכלו להחזיר לי את הכסף?

LOSS

I have lost . . .	'Ibadti et . . . ee-*bahd*-ti eht איבדתי את
my bag	hatik sheli hah-*tik* sheh-*lee* התיק שלי
my bracelet	hatsamid sheli hah-tsah-*mid* sheh-*lee* הצמיד שלי
my camera	hamatslemah sheli hah-mats-leh-*mah* sheh-*lee* המצלמה שלי
my car keys	maftekhot ha-mekhonit mahf-teh-*khot* hah-meh-kho-*nit* מפתחות המכונית
my driving licence	rishyon hanehigah sheli rish-*yon* hah-neh-hee-*gah* sheh-*lee* רשיון הנהיגה שלי
my insurance certificate	polisat ha-bitooakh sheli *poh*-lee-saht hab-bee-*too*-akh sheh-*lee* פוליסת הביטוח שלי
my jewellery	ha-takhshitim sheli hah-tahkh-shee-*tim* sheh-*lee* התכשיטים שלי
everything!	hakol! hah-*kol* הכל

THEFT

[See also 'Loss' above: the lists are interchangeable]

Someone has stolen . . .	**Mishehoo ganav et . . .** *mee-sheh-hoo gah-nahv* eht . . . מישהו גנב את
my car	**ha-mekhonit sheli** hah-meh-khoh-*nit* sheh-*lee* המכונית שלי
my car radio	**ha-radyo ba-mekhonit sheli** hah-*rahd*-yoh bah-meh-khoh-*nit* sheh-*lee* הרדיו במכונית שלי
my keys	**hamaftekhot sheli** hah-mahf-teh-*khot* sheh-*lee* המפתחות שלי
my money	**ha-kessef sheli** hah-*keh*-sef sheh-*lee* הכסף שלי
my necklace	**ha-sharsheret sheli** hah-shahr-*sheh*-ret sheh-*lee* השרשרת שלי
my passport	**ha-darkon sheli** hah-dahr-*kon* sheh-*lee* הדרכון שלי
my radio	**ha-radio sheli** hah-*rahd*-yoh sheh-*lee* הרדיו שלי
my tickets	**ha-kartisim sheli** hah-kahr-tee-*sim* sheh-*lee* הכרטיסים שלי
my travellers' cheques	**ha-travelers cheques sheli** hah-*trah*-veh-lers chehks sheh-*lee* הטראבלרס צ'קס שלי
my wallet	**ha-arnak sheli** hah-ahr-*nahk* sheh-*lee* הארנק שלי
my watch	**ha-sha'on sheli** hah-shah-*on* sheh-*lee* השעון שלי
my luggage	**ha-mizvadot sheli** hah-miz-vah-*dot* sheh-*lee* המזוודות שלי

LIKELY REACTIONS: key words to understand

Wait	**Khakeh (m)/khaki (f)**
	khah-*keh*/khah-*kee*
	חכה/חכי
When?	**Matay?**
	mah-*tye*?
	מתי?
Where?	**Eyfoh?**
	ehy-foh?
	איפה?
Name	**Shem?**
	shem?
	שם?
Address	**Ktovet?**
	ktoh-vet?
	כתובת?
I can't help you	**Ani lo yakhol la'azor lekha (m) lakh (f)**
	ah-*nee* loh yah-*khol* lah-ah-*zor* leh-*khah*/lahkh
	אני לא יכול לעזור לך
Please contact the police	**Tifneh (m.)/tifni (f.) la-mishtara bevakashah**
	teef-*neh* (m.)/teef-*nee* (f.) lah-mish-tah-*rah* beh-vah-kah-*shah*
	תפנה/תפני למשטרה בבקשה

The post office

ESSENTIAL INFORMATION

- To find a post office, see p.12.
- Look for this sign:

רשות הדואר

- Post offices are open from 8.00a.m. to 12.30p.m., and from 4.00p.m. to 6.00p.m. (except Saturdays). In larger towns there is usually a post office open until midnight.
- Post offices offer a range of services, from postage stamps and telephone jetons, to payments and bank accounts.
- In the main cities there are two kinds of letter-boxes: yellow – in the city area; red – all other destinations.

WHAT TO SAY

To England, please *[Hand letters, cards or parcels over the counter]*	**Le-angliyah bevakashah** leh-*ahn*-glee-yah beh-vah-kah-*shah* לאנגליה בבקשה
To Australia	**Le-ostralyah** leh-oss-*trahl*-yah לאוסטרליה
To the United States	**Le-amerikah** leh-ah-*meh*-ree-kah לאמריקה

[For other countries see p.149]

How much is . . .	**Kamah zeh . . .** *kah*-mah zeh כמה זה . . .
this parcel (to Canada)?	**ha-khavilah hazot (le-kanadah)?** hah-khah-vee-*lah* hah-*zot* (leh-*kah*-nah-dah) החבילה הזאת (לקנדה)?

a letter (to Australia)?	**mikhtav (le-ostralyah)?** meekh-*tahv* leh-oss-*trahl*-yah מכתב (לאוסטרליה)?
a postcard (to England)?	**glooyah (le-angliyah)** gloo-*yah* (leh-*ahn*-glee-yah) גלויה (לאנגליה)?
Air mail	**Do'ar avir** *doh*-ahr ah-*veer* דואר אוויר
Surface mail	**Do'ar ragil** *doh*-ahr rah-*gheel* דואר רגיל
One stamp, please	**Bool ekhad bevakashah** bool eh-*khahd* beh-vah-kah-*shah* בול אחד בבקשה
Two stamps	**Shney boolim** shnehy boo-*lim* שני בולים
One (fifty) Agorot stamp	**Bool ekhad shel (khamishim) agorot** bool eh-*khahd* shel (khah-mee-*shim*) ah-goh-*rot* בול אחד של (חמישים) אגורות
I'd like to send a telegram	**Ani rotseh lishloakh mikhtav** ah-*nee* roh-*tseh* lish-*loh*-ahkh mikh-*tahv* אני רוצה לשלוח מכתב

Telephoning

ESSENTIAL INFORMATION

- In order to make a telephone call from a public callbox you will
  need a jeton or (in city centres) a phone card. These are obtainable
  from post offices, special vending machines and street vendors.
  Callboxes usually have instructions on them in both Hebrew and
  English.
- There are telephones at post offices; telephone boxes in the street
  are silver and blue.
- Many shops, kiosks and coffee houses have counter-operated
  phones, although some will only let you make local phone calls.
- If you want to make a long-distance or international call without
  using jetons or phone cards, you can do so at the post office. The
  exchange will dial for you and direct you to a booth to take the call.
  Payment for the call is made afterwards at the same counter.
- To make local calls, just dial the number. To make calls outside the
  city limits dial the area code first (0, followed by one or two digits)
  and the number. To make international calls dial 00, then dial the
  country code and number.
- To call the UK dial 00–44, then the number (minus any initial zero
  on the area code).
- To call the USA dial 00–1, then the number.
- The telephone system in Israel is improving rapidly. In some areas,
  however, exchanges are still old-fashioned, and you may have to
  dial slowly, perhaps more than once, before you are successful.

WHAT TO SAY

Where can I make a telephone call?	**Me'eyfoh efshar le-hitkasher?** meh-*ehy*-foh ehf-*shahr* leh-hit-kah-*sher* מאיפה אפשר להתקשרד
Local/abroad	**Mekomi/le-khoots la-arets** meh-koh-*mee*/leh-*khoots* lah-*ah*-rets מקומי/לחוץ–לארץ

I'd like to call this number . . . *[show number]*	Ani rotseh (m.) /rotsah (f.) le-hitkasher la-mispar hah-zeh . . .
	ah-*nee*-roh-*tseh* (m.)/roh-*tsah* (f.) leh-hit-kah-*sher* lah-miss-*pahr* hah-*zeh*
	אני רוצה להתקשר למספר הזה . . .
in England	be-angliyah
	beh-*ahn*-glee-yah
	באנגליה
in Canada	be-kanadah
	beh-*kah*-nah-dah
	בקנדה
in the USA *[For other countries see p.149]*	be-artsot ha-brit
	beh-ahr-*tsot* hah-brit
	בארצות הברית
Can you dial it for me, please?	Tookhal (m.)/tookhlee (f.) le-khayeg li oto bevakashah?
	too-*khahl* (m.)/too-khlee (f.) leh-khah-*yeg* lee oh-*toh* beh-vah-kah-*shah*
	תוכל/י לחייג לי אותו בבקשה?
How much is it?	Kamah zeh?
	kah-mah zeh
	כמה זה?
Hallo!	Halo!
	hah-*loh*
	הלו!
May I speak to . . .	Efshar ledaber 'im . . .
	ehf-*shahr* leh-dah-*ber* eem . . .
	אפשר לדבר עם . . .
Extention . . .	Shlookhah . . .
	shloo-*khah*
	שלוחה . . .
I'm sorry, I don't speak Hebrew	Mitsta'er (m.)/mitsta'eret (f.) ani lo medaber (m.)/medaberet (f.) ivrit
	mits-tah-*ehr* (m.)/mits-tah-*eh*-ret (f.), Ah-*nee* loh meh-dah-*ber* (m.)/meh-dah-*beh*-ret (f.) eev-*rit*
	מצטער/ת אני לא מדבר/ת עברית

Do you speak English?	**Atah medaber (m.)/at medaberet (f.) anglit?** ah-*tah* meh-dah-*ber* (m.)/aht meh dah-*beh*-ret (f.) ahn-*glit* את/ה מדבר/ת אנגלית?
Thank you, I'll phone back	**Todah, ani etkasher bakhazarah** tot-*dah*, ah-*nee* eht-kah-*sher* bah-khah-zah-*rah* תודה, אני אתקשר בחזרה
Goodbye	**le-hitra'ot** leh-hit-rah-*ot* להתראות

LIKELY REACTIONS

That's (2) shekels	**Zeh (shney) shkalim** zeh (shnehy) shkah-*lim* זה (שני) שקלים
Cabin number (3)	**Tah mispar (shalosh)** tah miss-*pahr* (shah-*losh*) תא מספר (שלוש)

[For numbers see p.135]

Don't hang up	**Al tenatek (m)/al tenatki (f)** ahl teh-nah-*tek* (m)/ahl teh-nah-*tkee* (f) אל תנתק/י
I'm trying to connect you	**Ani menaseh (m.)/ menasah (f.) lekasher otkhem** ah-*nee* meh-nah-*seh* (m.)/meh-nah-sah (f.) leh-kah-*sher* oht-*khem* אני מנסה לקשר אתכם
You're through	**Dabroo** dah-*broo* דברו
There's a delay	**Yesh 'ikoov** yesh ee-*koov* יש עיכוב
I'll try again	**Ani anaseh shoov** ah-*nee* ah-nah-*seh* shoov אני אנסה שוב

Changing checks and money

ESSENTIAL INFORMATION

- For finding the way to the bank, see p.12.
- Money can be changed in banks and hotels.
- All banks, and most dealers, accept traveller's cheques and Eurocheques.
- Banks are usually open from 8.30a.m. to 12.30p.m. and from 4.00p.m. to 5.30p.m.
- Have your passport handy.

WHAT TO SAY

I'd like to cash ...	Ani rotseh (m.)/ rotsah (f.) lifrot ... ah-*nee* roh-*tseh* (m.)/ roh-tsah (f.) lee-*froht* ... אני רוצה לפרוט ...
this traveller's cheque	et ha-travelers chek ha-zeh eht hah-*trah*-veh-lers chek hah-*zeh* את הטראבלרס צ'ק הזה
these traveller's cheques	et ha-travelers cheks ha-eleh eht hah-*trah*-veh-lers cheks hah-eh-leh את הטראבלרס צ'קס האלה
I'd like to change this into shekels	Ani rotseh (m.)/rotsah (f.) le-hamir et zeh be-shkalim ah-*nee* roh-*tseh* (m.)/roh-tsah (f.) leh-hah-*meer* eht zeh beh-shkah-*lim* אני רוצה להמיר את זה בשקלים
Here's ...	Hineh ... *hee*-neh ... הנה ...
my banker's card	kartis ha-bank sheli kahr-*tiss* hah-*bahnk* sheh-*lee* כרטיס הבנק שלי
my credit card	kartis ha-ashray sheli kahr-*tiss* hah-ahsh-*rye* sheh-*lee* כרטיס האשראי שלי
my passport	ha-darkon sheli hah-dahr-*kon* sheh-*lee* הדרכון שלי

What's the rate of exchange?	**Mah sha'ar ha-khalifin?**
	mah *shah*-ahr hah-khah-lee-*fin*
	מה שער החליפין

LIKELY REACTIONS

Passport, please	**Darkon bevakasha**
	dahr-*kon* beh-vah-kah-*shah*
	דרכון בבקשה
Sign here	**Khatom (m.)/takhtemi (f.) kan**
	khah-*tom* (m.)/
	táhkh-teh-mee (f.) kahn
	חתום כאן
Your banker's card, please	**Et kartis habank shelkha (m.)/**
	shelakh (f.), bevakashah
	et kahr-*tiss* hah-*bahnk* shehl-*khah*
	(m.)/sheh-lahkh (f.) beh-vah-kah-*shah*
	את כרטיס הבנק שלך בבקשה
The rate is . . .	**Ha-sha'ar hoo . . .**
	hah-*shah*-ahr hoo
	השער הוא . . .

Car travel

ESSENTIAL INFORMATION

- For finding a filling station or garage, see p.14.
- Grades of petrol:
  normal (91 octane)
  super (96 octane)
- Petrol stations may be able to help with minor repairs or direct you to a mechanic.
- The equivalent of the AA/RAC in Israel is the MEMSI (Automobile and Touring club of Israel).
- Several companies – Magor, Shamgar, etc. – offer road repair services and towing insurance.

WHAT TO SAY
[For numbers see p. 135]

(9) litres of . .	**(tish'ah) liter . . .**
	(tish-*ah*) *lee*-ter
	. . . תשעה ליטר
(30) shekels of . .	**. . .be-(shloshim) shekel**
	beh-(shloh-*shim*) *sheh*-kel
	. . . ב(שלושים) שקל
standard (91)	**tish'im ve-ekhad**
	tish-*eem* veh-eh-*khahd*
	תשעים ואחד
super (96)	**tish'im ve-shesh**
	tish-*eem* veh-*shesh*
	תשעים ושש
diesel	**dizel**
	dee-zel
	דיזל
Fill the tank please	**Maleh, bevakashah**
	man-*leh*, beh-vah-kah-*shah*
	מלא, בבקשה

Will you check . . .	**Tivdok bevakashah et . . .** tiv-*dok* beh-vah-kah-*shah* eht תבדוק בבקשה את . . .
the oil?	**hashemen** hah-*sheh*-men השמן
the battery?	**ha-batariya** hah-bah-tah-*ree*-yah הבטריה
the radiator?	**ha-radyator** hah-rahd-*yah*-tor הרדיאטור
the tyres?	**ha-tsmigim** hah-tsmee-*ghim* הצמיגים
I've run out of petrol	**Nigmar li ha-delek** nig-*mahr* lee hah-*deh*-lek נגמר לי הדלק
May I borrow a can, please?	**Tookhal le-hash'il li meykhal bevakasha?** too-*khahl* leh-hahsh-*eel* lee mehy- *khahl* beh-vah-kah-*shah* תוכל להשאיל לי מיכל בבקשה?
My car has broken down	**Ha-mekhonit sheli nitke'ah** hah-meh-khoh-*neet* sheh-*lee* nit- keh-*ah* המכונית שלי נתקעה
My car won't start	**Ani lo matsliakh le-hatni'a** ah-*nee* loh mahts-*lee*-ahkh leh- haht-*nee*-ah אני לא מצליח להתניע
There's been an accident	**Kartah te'oonah** kahr-*tah* teh-oo-*nah* קרתה תאונה
I've lost my car keys	**'Ibadti et ha-maftekhot** ee-*bahd*-ti eht hah-mahf-teh-*khot* איבדתי את המפתחות
My car is . . .	**Ha-mekhonit . . .** hah-meh-khoh-*neet* המכונית . . .
two kilometres away	**shney kilometer mikan** shnehy kee-loh-*meh*-ter mee-*kahn* שני קילומטר מכאן

three kilometres away	**shlosha kilometer mikan**
	shloh-*shah* kee-loh-*meh*-ter mee-*kahn*
	שלושה קילומטר מכאן
Can you help me, please?	**Tookhal la'azor li, bevakashah?**
	too-*khahl* lah-ah-*zor* lee beh-vah-kah-*shah*
	תוכל לעזור לי בבקשה?
Do you do repairs?	**Atem ossim tikoonim?**
	ah-*tem* oh-*seem* tee-koo-*nim*
	אתם עושים תיקונים?
I have a puncture	**Yesh li pancher**
	yesh lee *pahn*-cher
	יש לי פנצ'ר
I have a broken windscreen	**Nishberah li shmashah**
	nish-beh-*rah* lee shmah-*shah*
	נשברה לי שמשה
I think the problem is here . . . *[point]*	**Ani khoshev (m.)/khoshevet (f.) sheha-be'ayah kan**
	ah-*nee* khoh-*shev* (m.)/khoh-*sheh*-vet (f.) shehah-beh-ah-*yah* kahn
	אני חושב/ת שהבעיה כאן
I don't know what's wrong	**Ani lo yode'a mah ha-be'ayah**
	ah-*nee* loh yoh-*deh*-ah mah hah-beh-ah-*yah*
	אני לא יודע מה הבעיה
Can you repair the fault?	**Tookhal letaken et ha-takalah?**
	too-*khahl* leh-tah-*ken* eht hah-tah-kah-*lah*
	תוכל לתקן את התקלה?
Can you come and look?	**Tookhal lavo lehistakel?**
	too-*khahl* lah-*voh* leh-hiss-tah-*kel*
	תוכל לבוא להסתכל?
Can you estimate the cost?	**Tookhal le-ha'arikh et ha-mekhir?**
	too-*khahl* leh-hah-ah-*rikh* eht hah-meh-*kheer*
	תוכל להעריך את המחיר?
Can you write it down?	**Tookhal likhtov et zeh?**
	too-*khahl* likh-*tov* eht zeh
	תוכל לכתוב את זה?

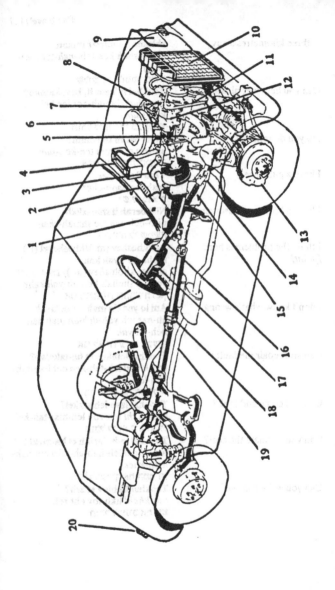

1	windscreen wipers	magavim	mah-gah-*vim*	מגבים
2	fuses	fyoozim	*fyoo*-zim	פיוזים
3	heater	khimoom	khee-*moom*	חימום
4	battery	batariyah	bah-tah-ree-yah	בטריה
5	engine	mano'a	mah-*noh*-ah	מנוע
6	fuel pump	mash'evat delek	mahsh-eh-*vaht deh*-lek	משאבת דלק
7	starter motor	starter	*stahr*-ter	סטרטר
8	carburettor	karburator	kahr-boo-*rah-tor*	קרבורטור
9	lights	orot	oh-*rot*	אורות
10	radiator	radyator	rahd-*yah*-tor	רדיאטור
11	fan belt	khagorah	khah-goh-*rah*	חגורה
12	generator	alternator	ahl-ter-*nah*-tor	אלטרנטור
13	brakes	ma'atsorim	mah-ah-tsoh-*rim*	מעצורים
14	clutch	klatch	*klahtch*	קלאץ
15	gear box	tevat hilookhim	teh-*vaht* hee-loo-*khim*	תבת הילוכים
16	steering	hegeh	*heh*-gheh	הגה
17	ignition	hatsatah	hah-tsah-*tah*	הצתה
18	transmission	timsoret	tim-*soh*-ret	תמסורת
19	exhaust	egzoz	eg-*zoz*	אגזוז
20	indicator	vinker	*ween*-ker	וינקר

Do you accept these coupons?	**Atah mekabel et ha-tlooshim ha-eleh?**
	ah-*tah* meh-kah-*bel* eht hah-tloo-*shim* hah-*eh*-leh
	אתה מקבל את התלושים האלה?
How long will the repair take?	**Kamah zman yimashekh ha-tikoon?**
	kah-mah zmahn yee-mah-*shekh* hah-tee-*koon*
	כמה זמן יימשך התיקון?
When will the car be ready?	**Matay tihyeh ha-mekhonit mookhanah?**
	mah-*tye* tee-hee-*yeh* hah-meh-khoh-*nit* moo-khah-*nah*
	מתי תהיה המכונית מוכנה?
Can I see the bill?	**Efshar lir'ot et ha-kheshbon?**
	ehf-*shahr* leer-*oht* eht hah-khesh-*bon*
	אפשר לראות את החשבון?
This is my insurance document	**Zot ha-polisah sheli**
	zoht hah-*poh*-lee-sah sheh-*li*
	זאת הפוליסה שלי

HIRING A CAR

Can I hire a car?	**Efshar liskor mekhonit?**
	ehf-*shahr* liss-*kor* meh-khoh-*nit*
	אפשר לשכור מכונית?
I need a car . . .	**Ani tsarikh (m)/ tsrikhah (f) mekhonit . . .**
	ah-*nee* tsah-*rikh* (m)/tsree-*khah* (f) meh-khoh-*nit*
	אני צריך/צריכה מכונית . . .
for two people	**le-shney anashim**
	leh-*shnehy* ah-nah-*shim*
	לשני אנשים
for five people	**le-khamishah anashim**
	leh-khah-mee-*shah* ah-nah-*shim*
	לחמישה אנשים
for one day	**le-yom ekhad**
	leh-*yohm* eh-*khahd*
	ליום אחד

for five days	**le-khamishah yamin** leh-khah-mee-*shah* yah-*mim* לחמישה ימים
for a week	**le-shavoo'a** leh-shah-*voo*-ah לשבוע
Can you write down . . .	**Tookhal** (m)/**tookhli** (f) **likhtov et . . .** too-*khahl* (m)/tookh-*lee* (f) leekh-tov eht תוכל/י לכתוב את . . .
the deposit to pay?	**skhoom ha-eravon?** skhoom hah-eh-rah-*von* סכום הערבון
the charge per kilometre?	**ha-mekhir le-kilometer?** hah-meh-*khir* leh-kee-loh-*meh*-ter המחיר לקילומטר
the daily charge?	**ha-mekhir le yom?** hah-meh-*khir* leh-*yom* המחיר ליום
the cost of insurance?	**mekhir ha-bitoo'akh?** meh-*khir* hah-bee-*too*-ahkh מחיר הביטוח
Can I leave the car in Jerusalem	**Efshar le-hash'ir et ha-mekhonit be-yerooshalayim?** ehf-*shahr* leh-hahsh-*eer* eht hah-meh-khoh-*nit* beh-yeh-roo-shah-*lah*-yim אפשר להשאיר את המכונית בירושלים
What documents do I need?	**Eyzeh mismakhim ani tsarikh?** ehy-*zeh* miss-mah-khim ah-*nee* tsah-*rikh* איזה מסמכים אני צריך

LIKELY REACTIONS

I don't do repairs	**Ani lo oseh tikoonim** ah-*nee* loh oh-*seh* tee-koo-*nim* אני לא עושה תיקונים
Where's your car?	**Eyfo ha-mekhonit shelkha** (m.)/**shelakh** (f.)? ehy-*foh* hah-meh-khoh-*nit* shel-*khah* (m.)/sheh-lakh (f.) איפה המכונית שלך

What make is it?	**Eyzeh soog hee?** *ehy*-zeh soog hee איזה סוג היא?
Come back (tomorrow/on Monday)	**Takhazor (m.)/takhzeri (f.)** **(makhar/be-yom sheni)** tah-khah-*zor* (m.)/tahkh-zeh-*ree* (f.) (mah-*khahar*/beh-yom sheh-*nee*) תחזור תחזרי (מחר/ביום שני)

[For days of the week, see p.142]

We don't hire cars	**Anakhnoo loh maskirim rekhev** ah-*nahkh*-noo loh muss-kee-*rim* *reh*-khev אנחנו לא משכירים רכב
Your driving licence, please	**Et rishyon ha-nehigah shelkha** **(m)/sheh-lakh (f) bevakasha** eht rish-*yon* hah-neh-hee-*gah* shel-*khah* (m.)/sheh-lakh (f.), beh-vah-kah-*shah* את רשיון הנהיגה שלך בבקשה
The mileage is unlimited	**Mispar hakilometrin lo moogbal** miss-*pahr* hah-kee-loh-*met*-rim loh moog-*bahl* מספר הקילומטרים לא מוגבל

Public transportation

ESSENTIAL INFORMATION

- For finding the way to a bus station, a bus stop, the railway station and a taxi rank, see p.11.
- The train service in Israel is not very efficient, except for the Tel-Aviv to Haifa line. In most cases bus travel will be more frequent, and faster.
- There is a very extensive network of buses throughout the country, most of them operated by the EGED company (in Tel-Aviv, the major company is DAN). Many buses (and almost all those on inter-city routes) have air-conditioning and are comfortable even on hot summer days.
- Bus prices are fixed and subsidized. You can choose between a single ticket, a 'carnet' of 25 rides, and a monthly ticket (in the big cities), that enables you to board as many buses as you wish in the city during the month. All tickets are bought from the bus driver or from vendors in main bus stations.
- **Sheroot:** A sheroot (the name means 'service') is a shared taxi that travels a fixed route, for which you pay a fixed rate. The cars queue at taxi ranks, and as soon as a vehicle is full, it sets off. Destinations are sometimes marked on signs at the ranks or called out by the drivers. You can get off at any point along the route by asking the driver to stop. Make sure this is a sheroot by asking 'sheroot?', before you get in.
- Taxis can be picked up at ranks or flagged down in the street. They all have meters, which by law must be in working order. It is wise to make sure the driver has turned the meter on before setting out. At the end of the journey pay what is on the meter. A tip is not necessary unless some special service has been rendered.
- Some drivers may offer a 'deal' – a fixed price for the journey, with the meter off. This is illegal inside the city limits, and anyway, if you are not sure about the estimated cost of the journey, do not accept.

WHAT TO SAY

Where does the bus (for Eilat) leave from?	**Me'eyfoh yotseh ha'otobus (le-eylat)?** meh-*ehy*-foh yoh-*tseh* hah-*oh*-toh-boos (leh-ehy-*laht*) מאיפה יוצא האוטובוס (לאילת)?
At what time does the bus leave (for Safed)?	**Matay yotseh ha-otoboos (le-tsfat)?** mah-*tye* yoh-*tseh* hah-*oh*-toh-boos (leh-*tsfaht*) מתי יוצא האוטובוס (לצפת)?
Is this the bus (for Beer-sheba)	**Zeh ha-otoboos (le-be'er sheva)?** zeh hah-*oh*-toh-boos (leh-beh-*ehr sheh*-vah) זה האוטובוס (לבאר שבע)?
Where does the train (for Haifa) leave from?	**Me'eyfoh yotset ha-rakevet (le-kheyfah)?** meh-*ehy*-foh yoh-*tseht* hah-rah-*keh*-vet (leh-khehy-*fah*) מאיפה יוצאת הרכבת (לחיפה)?
At what time does the train leave (for Haifa)?	**Matay yotset ha-rakevet (le-kheyfah)?** mah-*tye* yoh-*tseht* hah-rah-*keh*-vet (leh-khehy-*fah*) מתי יוצאת הרכבת (לחיפה)?
Do I have to change?	**Ani tsarikh (m.)/tsrikhah (f.) le-hakhalif?** ah-*nee* tsah-*reekh* (m.) tsree-*khah* (f.) leh-hah-khah-*lif* להחליף? אני צריך/צריכה
Where does . . . leave from?	**Me-eyfoh yotseh . . .** meh-*ehy*-foh yoh-*tseh* מאיפה יוצא . . .
the bus	**ha-otoboos?** hah-*oh*-toh-boos האוטובוס?
the train	**ha-rakevet?** hah-rah-*keh*-vet הרכבת?
the sheroot	**ha-sheroot?** hah-sheh-*root* השרות?

for the airport	**le-sdeh ha-te'oofah?**
	leh-*sdeh*-hah-teh-oo-*fah*
	לשדה התעופה?
for the old city	**la-'ir ha-atika?**
	lah-*eer* hah-ah-tee-*kah*
	לעיר העתיקה?
for the beach	**la-khof?**
	lah-*khohf*
	לחוף?
for the market	**la-shook?**
	lah-*shook*
	לשוק?
for the central bus station	**la-takhanah ha-merkazit?**
	lah-tah-khah-*nah* hah-mer-kah-*zit*
	לתחנה המרכזית?
for the town centre	**le-merkaz ha-'ir?**
	leh-mehr-*kahz* hah-*eer*
	למרכז העיר?
for the town hall	**la-'iryah?**
	lah-eer-*yah*
	לעירייה?
for the church	**la-knessiyah?**
	lah-kneh-see-*yah*
	לכנסיה?
for the synagogue	**le-beyt ha-knesset?**
	leh-*behyt* hah-*kneh*-set
	לבית הכנסת?
for the swimming pool	**la-brekhah**
	lah-breh-*khah*
	לבריכה?
for the sea shore	**la-yam?**
	lah-*yahm*
	לים?
Is this the bus for the market place?	**Zeh ha-otoboos la-shook?**
	zeh hah-*oh*-toh-boos lah-*shook*
	זה האוטובוס לשוק?
Is this the sheroot for Tel-Aviv?	**Zeh ha-sheroot le-Tel-Aviv?**
	zeh hah-sheh-*root* leh-tel-ah-*viv*
	זה השרות לתל–אביב?
Where can I get a taxi?	**Eyfoh efshar le-hassig taxi?**
	ehy-*foh* ehf-*shahr* leh-hah-*sig tah*-ksi
	איפה אפשר להשיג טקסי?

Can you put me off at the right stop, please?	**Tookhal le-hagid li eyfoh laredet?**
	too-*khahl* leh-hah-*ghid* lee *ehy*-foh lah-*reh*-det
	תוכל להגיד לי איפה לרדת
A single ticket	**Kartis ekhad**
	kahr-*tiss* eh-*khahd*
	כרטיס אחד
A return	**Kartis halokh va-shov**
	kahr-*tiss* hah-*lokh* vah-*shohv*
	כרטיס הלוך ושוב
One adult	**Mevoogar ekhad**
	meh-voo-*gahr* eh-*khahd*
	מבוגר אחד
Two adults	**Shney mevoogarim**
	shnehy meh-voo-gah-*rim*
	שני מבוגרים
and one child	**ye-yeled ekhad**
	veh-*yeh*-led eh-*khahd*
	וילד אחד
and two children	**ve-shney yeladim**
	veh-*shnehy* yeh-lah-*dim*
	ושני ילדים
How much is it?	**Kamah zeh?**
	kah-mah zeh
	כמה זהז

LIKELY REACTIONS

Over there	**Sham**
	shahm
	שם
Here	**Kan**
	kahn
	כאן
Platform (1)	**Ratsif (ekhad)**
	rah-*tsif* (eh-*khahd*)
	רציף (אחד)
(At 4) o'clock	**Be-sha'ah (arbah)**
	beh-shah-*ah* (*ahr*-bah)
	בשעה (ארבע)

[For times, see p.139]

Change (at Tel-Aviv)	**Takhalif (m.)/Takhalifi (f.)** **(be-Tel-Aviv)** tah-khah-*lif* (m.)/tah-khah-*lee*-fee (f.) (beh-tel-ah-*viv*) תחליף/תחליפי בתל־אביב
Change (at the market)	**Takhalif (m.)/** **Takhalifi (f.) (ba-shook)** tah-khah-*lif* (m.)/ tah-khah-*lee*-fee (f.) (bah-*shook*) תחליף/תחליפי בשוק
This is your stop	**Zot ha-takhanah shelkha (m.)/** **shelakh (f.)** zoht hah-tah-khah-*nah* shel-*khah* (m.)/ sheh-lakh (f.) זאת התחנה שלך
Get off here	**Red (m.)/redi (f.) kan** red (m.)/reh-*dee* (f.) kahn רד/י כאן

Leisure

ESSENTIAL INFORMATION

- For finding the way to a place of entertainment see p.11.
- For times of day, see p.139.
- All daily newspapers (like the *Jerusalem Post*) publish a list of films, plays, museums and other entertainment each day.

WHAT TO SAY

At what time does . . . open?	**Be-eyzeh sha'ah niftakh . . .** beh-*ehy*-zeh shah-*ah* nif-*tahkh* . . . באיזה שעה נפתח
the art gallery	**ha-galeryah?** hah-gah-*lehr*-yah הגלריה?
the cinema	**ha-kolno'a?** hah-kol-*noh*-ah הקולנוע?
the concert hall	**oolam ha-kontsertim?** oo-*lahm* hah-kon-*tsehr*-tim אולם הקונצרטים?
the disco	**ha-diskotek?** hah-diss-koh-*tek* הדיסקוטק?
the museum	**ha-moze'on?** hah-moh-*zeh*-on המוזיאון?
the night club	**mo'adon ha-laylah?** moh-ah-*don* hah-*lye*-lah מועדון הלילה?
the sports stadium	**ha-'itstadyon?** hah-its-tahd-*yon* האיצטדיון?
the swimming pool	**brekhat ha-skhiyah?** breh-*khaht* hah-skhee-*yah* ברכת השחיה?
the theatre	**ha-te'atron?** hah-teh-aht-*ron* התיאטרון?

the zoo	**gan ha-khayot?**
	gahn hah-khah-*yot*
	גן החיות?
At what time does . . . close?	**Be-eyzeh sha'ah nisgar . . .**
[See above list]	beh-*ehy*-zeh shah-*ah* niss-*gahr*
	באיזה שעה נסגר . . .
At what time does . . . start?	**Be-eyzeh sha'ah matkhil . . .**
	beh-ehy-*zeh* shah-*ah* maht-*kheel*
	באיזה שעה מתחיל . . .
the cabaret	**ha-kabaret?**
	hah-kah-bah-*rett*
	הקברט?
the concert	**ha-kontsert?**
	hah-kohn-*tsehrt*
	הקונצרט?
the film	**ha-seret?**
	hah-*seh*-ret
	הסרט?
the match	**ha-miskhak?**
	hah-miss-*khahk*
	המשחק?
the play	**ha-hatsagah?**
	hah-hah-tsah-*gah*
	ההצגה?
the race	**ha-merots?**
	hah-meh-*rohts*
	המרוץ?
How much is it . . .	**Kamah zeh . . .**
	kah-mah zeh
	כמה זה . . .
for an adult?	**le-mevoogar?**
	leh-meh-voo-*gahr*
	למבוגר?
for a child?	**le-yeled?**
	leh-*yeh*-led
	לילד?
Two adults, please	**Shney mevoogarim bevakashah**
	shnehy meh-voo-gah-*rim* beh-vah-
	kah-*shah*
	שני מבוגרים בבקשה
Three children, please	**Shloshah yeladim bevakashah**
	shloh-*shah* yeh-lah-*dim* beh-vah-
	kah-*shah*
	שלושה ילדים בבקשה

Stalls/circle	**Oolam/yatsi'a** oo-lahm/yah-*tsee*-ah אולם/יציע
Do you have . . .	**Yesh lakhem . . .** yesh lah-*khem* . . . יש לכם
a programme?	**tokhniyah?** tokh-nee-*yah* תוכניה?
a guide book?	**madrikh?** mahd-*rikh* מדריך
Where's the toilet, please?	**Eyfoh ha-sherootim bevakashah?** ehy-*foh* hah-sheh-roo-*tim* beh-vah-kah-*shah* איפה השרותים בבקשה?
Where's the cloakroom?	**Eyfoh ha-meltakhah?** ehy-*foh* hah-mel-tah-*khah* איפה המלתחה?
I would like lessons in . . .	**Ani rotseh lilmod . . .** ah-*nee* roh-*tseh* lill-*mohd* . . . אני רוצה ללמוד
skiing	**ski** ski סקי
sailing	**sheyt mifrasiyot** shehyt mee-frah-see-*yot* שיט מפרשיות
water-skiing	**ski mayim** ski *mah*-yim סקי מים
sub-aqua diving	**tslilah** tslee-*lah* צלילה
windsurfing	**galshan rooakh** gahl-*shahn roo*-ahkh גלשן רוח
Can I hire . . .	**Efshar liskor . . .** ehf-*shahr* liss-*kohr* . . . אפשר לשכור
some skis?	**miglashayim?** mig-lah-*shah*-yim מגלשיים?

a boat?	**sirah?**
	see-rah
	סירה?
a fishing rod?	**khakah?**
	khah-*kah*
	חכה?
a deck chair?	**kisseh noakh?**
	kee-*seh noh*-ahkh
	כסא נוח?
a sun umbrella?	**shimshiyah?**
	shim-shee-*yah*
	שמשיה?
the necessary equipment?	**et ha-tsiyood ha-daroosh?**
	eht hah-tsee-*yood* hah-dah-*roosh*
	את הציוד הדרוש?
How much is it . . .	**Kamah zeh . . .**
	kah-mah zeh
	כמה זה . . .
per day/per hour?	**le-yom/le-sha'ah?**
	leh-*yom*/leh-shah-ah
	ליום/לשעה?
Do I need a licence?	**Ani tsarikh** (m.)/**tsrikhah** (f.) **rishayon?**
	ah-*nee* tsah-*rikh* (m.)/tsree-khah (f.) ree-shah-*yon*
	אני צריך צריכה רשיון?

Asking if things are allowed

Excuse me, please	**Slakh (m)/silkhi (f) lee, bevakashah** slahkh (m)/seel-*khi* lee, beh-vah-kah-*shah* סלח/י לי בבקשה
Can one ...	**Efshar ...** ehf-*shahr* ... אפשר
camp here?	**la-assot kan kemping?** lah-ah-*sot* kahn *kem*-ping לעשות כאן קמפינג?
come in?	**le-hikaness?** leh-hee-kah-*ness* להכנס?
dance here?	**lirkod kan?** leer-*kohd* kahn לרקוד כאן?
fish here?	**ladoog kan?** lah-*doog* kahn לדוג כאן?
get a drink here?	**le-kabel kan mashehoo lishtot?** leh-kah-*bell* kahn *mah*-sheh-hoo lish-*tot* לקבל כאן משהו לשתות?
get out this way?	**latset derekh kan?** lah-*tset deh*-rekh kahn לצאת דרך כאן?
get something to eat here?	**lekabel mashehoo le-ekhol kan?** leh-kah-*bel mah*-sheh-hoo leh-eh-*khol* kahn לקבל משהו לאכול כאן?
leave one's things here?	**le-hash'ir kan et ha-dvarim?** leh-hahsh-*eer* kahn eht hah-dvah-*rim* להשאיר כאן את הדברים?
look around here?	**le-histakel misaviv?** leh-hiss-tah-*kel* mee-sah-*viv* להסתכל מסביב?

park here?	**lakhanot kan?**
	lah-khah-*not* kahn
	לחנות כאן
sit here?	**lashevet kan?**
	lah-*sheh*-vet kahn
	לשבת כאן
smoke here?	**le-ashen kan?**
	leh-ah-*shen* kahn
	לעשן כאן
swim here?	**liskhot kan?**
	liss-*khot* kahn
	לשחות כאן
take photos here?	**letsalem kan?**
	leh-tsah-*lem* kahn
	לצלם כאן
telephone here?	**le-hitkasher mikan?**
	leh-hit-kah-*sher* mee-*kahn*
	להתקשר מכאן
wait here?	**le-khakot kan?**
	leh-khah-*kot* kahn
	לחכות כאן

LIKELY REACTIONS

Yes, certainly	**Ken, betakh**
	ken, *beh*-tahkh
	כן, בטח
No, certainly not	**Lo, beshoom ofen**
	loh, beh-*shoom oh*-fen
	לא, בשום אופן
I think so	**Ani khoshev (m.)/**
	khoshevet (f.) sheken
	ah-*nee* khoh-*shev* (m.)/
	khoh-sheh-vet (f.) sheh-*ken*
	אני חושב שכן
Of course	**Vaday/betakh**
	vah-*dye*/*beh*-tahkh
	ודאי/בטח
Yes, but be careful	**Ken, aval tizaher**
	ken, ah-*vahl* tee-zah-*herr*
	כן, אבל תזהר

134/Asking if things are allowed

I don't think so   **Ani khoshev shelo**
ah-*nee* khoh-*shev* sheh-*loh*
אני חושב שלא

Not normally   **Bederekh klal lo**
beh-*deh*-rekh klahl loh
בדרך כלל לא

Sorry   **Mitsta'er** (m.)/**mitsta'eret** (f.)
mits-tah-*ehr* (m.)/mits-tah-*eh*-ret (f.)
מצטער/ת

Reference

NUMBERS

Cardinal numbers

● All nouns in Hebrew have a gender. They are either masculine or feminine. 'A chair' (kee-*seh*) is masculine. 'Hope' (tik-*vah*) is feminine. All cardinal numbers from 1 to 19 have two versions conforming to this basic division. Nowadays many people prefer using just one – the shorter 'feminine' version – even while counting 'masculine' objects, especially when counting objects from 11 to 19. These numbers are therefore given in the more common version only.

0	**efes**	*eh*-fess
		אפס
1	**ekhad (m)/akhat (f)**	eh-*khahd* (m)/ah-*khaht* (f)
		אחד/אחת
2	**shnayim/shtayim**	*shnah*-yim/*shtah*-yim
		שניים/שתיים
3	**shloshah/shalosh**	shloh-*shah*/shah-*losh*
		שלושה/שלוש
4	**arba'ah/arbah**	ahr-bah-*ah*/*ahr*-bah
		ארבעה/ארבע
5	**khamishah/khamesh**	khah-mee-*shah*/khah-*mesh*
		חמישה/חמש
6	**shishah/shesh**	shee-*shah*/shesh
		ששה/שש
7	**shiv'ah/shevah**	shiv-*ah*/sheh-*vah*
		שבעה/שבע
8	**shmonah/shmoneh**	shmoh-*nah*/shmoh-neh
		שמונה/שמונה
9	**tish'ah/teshah**	tish-*ah*/*teh*-shah
		תשעה/תשע
10	**asarah/esser**	ah-sah-*rah*/*eh*-ser
		עשרה/עשר
11	**akhat esreh**	ah-*khaht* ess-*reh*
		אחת עשרה
12	**shtem esreh**	shtehm ess-*rek*
		שתים עשרה
13	**shlosh esreh**	shlohsh ess-*reh*
		שלוש עשרה

14	**arbah esreh**	ahr-*bah* ess-*reh* ארבע עשרה
15	**khamesh esreh**	khah-*mesh* ess-*reh* חמש עשרה
16	**shesh esreh**	shesh ess-*reh* שש עשרה
17	**shvah esreh**	shvah ess-*reh* שבע עשרה
18	**shmoneh esreh**	shmoh-*neh* ess-*reh* שמונה עשרה
19	**tshah esreh**	chah ess-*reh* תשע עשרה
20	**esrim**	ess-*rim* עשרים
21	**esrim ve-ekhad**	ess-*rim* veh-eh-*khahd* עשרים ואחד
22	**esrim ve-shtayim**	ess-*rim* veh-*shtah*-yim עשרים ושתיים
23	**esrim ve-shalosh**	ess-*rim* veh-shah-*losh* עשרים ושלוש
24	**esrim ve-arbah**	ess-*rim* veh-*ahr*-bah עשרים וארבע
25	**esrim ve-khamesh**	ess-*rim* veh-khah-*mesh* עשרים וחמש
30	**shloshim**	shloh-*shim* שלושים
35	**shloshim ve-khamesh**	shloh-*shim* veh-khah-*mesh* שלושים וחמש
40	**arba'im**	ahr-bah-*eem* ארבעים
45	**arba'im ve-khamesh**	ahr-bah-*eem* veh-khah-*mesh* ארבעים וחמש
50	**khamishim**	khah-mee-*shim* חמישים
55	**khamishim ve-khamesh**	khah-mee-*shim* veh-khah-*mesh* חמישים וחמש
60	**shishim**	shee-*shim* שישים
65	**shishim ve-khamesh**	shee-*shim* veh-khah-*mesh* שישים וחמש
70	**shiv'im**	shiv-*eem* שבעים

75	shiv'im ve-khamesh	shiv-*eem* veh-khah-*mesh*	שבעים וחמש
80	shmonim	shmoh-*nim*	שמונים
85	shmonim ve-khamesh	shmoh-*nim* veh-khah-mesh	שמונים וחמש
90	tish'im	tish-*eem*	תשעים
95	tish'im ve-khamesh	tish-*eem* veh-khah-*mesh*	תשעים וחמש
100	me'ah	meh-*ah*	מאה
105	me'ah ve-khamesh	meh-*ah* veh-khah-*mesh*	מאה וחמש
110	me'ah ve-eser	meh-*ah* veh-*eh*-ser	מאה ועשר
115	me'ah ve-khamesh esreh	meh-*ah* veh-khah-*mesh*-ess-*reh*	מאה וחמש עשרה
125	me'ah esrim ve-khamesh	meh-*ah* ess-*rim* veh-khah-*mesh*	מאה עשרים וחמש
200	maatayim	mah-*tah*-yim	מאתיים
205	maatayim ve-khamesh	mah-*tah*-yim veh-khah-*mesh*	מאתיים וחמש
215	maatayim ve-khamesh esreh	mah-*tah*-yim veh-khah-*mesh* ess-*reh*	מאתיים וחמש עשרה
300	shlosh me'ot	shlosh meh-*oht*	שלוש מאות
400	arbah-me'ot	ahr-*bah* meh-*oht*	ארבע מאות
500	khamesh me'ot	khah-*mesh* meh-*oht*	חמש מאות
600	shesh me'ot	shesh meh-*oht*	שש מאות
700	shvah me'ot	shvah meh-*oht*	שבע מאות
800	shmoneh me'ot	shmoh-*neh* meh-*oht*	שמונה מאות
900	tshah me'ot	chah meh-*oht*	תשע מאות
1000	elef	*eh*-leff	אלף

2000	**alpayim**	ahl-*pah*-yim אלפיים
5000	**khameshet alafim**	khan-*meh*-shet ah-lah-*fim* חמשת אלפים
10,000	**aseret alafim**	ah-*seh*-ret ah-lah-*fim* עשרת אלפים
100,000	**me'ah elef**	meh-*ah* eh-leff מאה אלף
1,000,000	**milyon**	mill-*yon* מיליון

Ordinal numbers

1st	**rishon** (m.)/**rishonah** (f.)	ree-*shon* (m.)/ ree-shoh-*nah* (f.) ראשון/ראשונה
2nd	**sheni/shniyah**	sheh-*nee*/shnee-*yah* שני/שניה
3rd	**shlishi/shlishit**	shlee-*shee*/shlee-*sheet* שלישי/שלישית
4th	**revi'I/revi'it**	reh-vee-*ee*/reh-vee-*it* רביעי/רביעית
5th	**khamishi/khamishit**	khah-mee-*shee*/khah-mee *sheet* חמישי/חמישית
6th	**shishi/shishit**	shee-*shee*/shee-*sheet* שישי/שישית
7th	**shvi'i/shvi'it**	shvee-*ee*/shvee-*it* שביעי/שביעית
8th	**shmini/shminit**	shmee-*nee*/shmee-*nit* שמיני/שמינית
9th	**tshi'i/tshi'it**	chee-*ee*/chee-*it* תשיעי/תשיעית
10th	**asiri/asirit**	ah-see-*ree*/ah-see-*rit* עשירי/עשירית
11th	**akhad asar**	ah-*khahd* ah-*sahr* אחד עשר
12th	**shneym asar**	shnehym ah-*sahr* שנים עשר

TIME

What time is it?	**mah ha-sha'ah?**
	mah hah-shah-*ah*
	מה השעה?
It's . . .	**Ha-sha'ah** (lit. – 'the hour is . . .')
	hah-shah-*ah* . . .
	. . . השעה
one o'clock	**akhat**
	ah-*khaht*
	אחת
two o'clock	**shtayim**
	shtah-yim
	שתיים
three o'clock	**shalosh**
	shah-*losh*
	שלוש
four o'clock in the morning	**arbah ba-boker**
	ahr-bah bah-*boh*-ker
	ארבע בבוקר
in the afternoon	**akharey ha-tsohorayim**
	ah-khah-*rehy* hah-tsoh-hoh-*rah*-yim
	אחרי הצהריים
in the evening	**ba-erev**
	bah-*eh*-rev
	בערב
at night	**ba-laylah**
	bah-*lye*-lah
	בלילה
It's . . .	**Ha-sha'ah . . .**
	hah-shah-*ah*
	. . . השעה
noon	**tsohorayim**
	tsoh-hoh-*rah*-yim
	צהריים
half-past twelve	**shteym esreh va-khetsi**
	shtehym ess-*reh* vah-*kheh*-tsi
	שתים עשרה וחצי
midnight	**khatsot**
	khah-*tsot*
	חצות

It's . . .

Ha-sha'ah . . .
hah-shah-*ah*
השעה

five past five

khamesh ve-khamishah
khah-*mesh* veh-khah-mee-*shah*
חמש וחמישה

ten past five

khamesh ve-asarah
khah-*mesh* veh-ah-sah-*rah*
חמש ועשרה

a quarter past five

khamesh va-revah
khah-*mesh* vah-*reh*-vah
חמש ורבע

twenty past five

khamesh ve-esrim
khah-*mesh* veh-ess-*rim*
חמש ועשרים

half-past five

khamesh va-khetsi
khah-*mesh* vah-*kheh*-tsi
חמש וחצי

twenty-five to six

esrim va-khamishah le-shesh
ess-*rim* vah-khah-mee-*shah* leh-*shesh*
עשרים וחמישה לשש

twenty to six

esrim le-shesh
ess-*rim* leh-*shesh*
עשרים לשש

a quarter to six

revah le-shesh
reh-vah leh-*shesh*
רבע לשש

ten to six

asarah le-shesh
ah-sah-*rah* leh-*shesh*
עשרה לשש

five to six

khamishah le-shesh
khah-mee-*shah* leh-*shesh*
חמישה לשש

At what time . . . (does the bus leave?)

Be-eyzeh sha'ah . . . (yotseh ha-otoboos?)
beh-*ehy*-zeh shah-*ah* . . . (yoh-*tseh* hah-oh-toh-*boos*)
(באיזה שעה (יוצא האוטובוס

At . . .	Be . . .
	beh
	ב . . .
13.00	**shlosh esreh**
	shlosh ess-*reh*
	שלוש עשרה
14.05	**arbah esreh ve-khamishah**
	ahr-*bah* ess-*reh* veh-khah-mee-*shah*
	ארבע עשרה וחמישה
15.10	**khamesh esreh ve-asarah**
	khah-*mesh* ess-*reh* veh-ah-sah-*rah*
	חמש עשרה ועשרה
16.15	**shesh esreh va-revah**
	shesh ess-*reh* vah-*reh*-vah
	שש עשרה ורבע
17.20	**shvah-esreh esrim**
	shvah ess-*reh* ess-*rim*
	שבע עשרה עשרים
18.25	**shmoneh esreh esrim ve-khamesh**
	shmoh-*neh* ess-*reh* ess-*rim* veh-khah-*mesh*
	שמונה עשרה עשרים וחמש
19.30	**tshah esreh shloshim**
	tshah ess-*reh* shloh-*shim*
	תשע עשרה שלושים
20.35	**esrim shloshim ve-khamesh**
	ess-*rim* shloh-*shim* veh-khah-*mesh*
	עשרים שלושים וחמש
21.40	**esrim ve-ekhad arba'im**
	ess-*rim* veh-eh-*khahd* ahr-bah-*eem*
	עשרים ואחד ארבעים
22.45	**esrim oo-shtayim arba'im ve-khamesh**
	ess-*rim* oo-*shtah*-yim ahr-bah-*eem*-veh-khah-*mesh*
	עשרים ושתיים ארבעים וחמש
23.50	**esrim ve-shalosh khamishim**
	ess-*rim* veh-shah-*losh* khah-mee-*shim*
	עשרים ושלוש חמישים
00.55	**efes khamishim ve-khamesh**
	eh-fess khah-mee-*shim* veh-khah-*mesh*
	אפס חמישים וחמש

in ten minutes	**od eser dakot**
	ohd *eh*-ser dah-*kot*
	עוד עשר דקות
in a quarter of an hour	**od revah sha'ah**
	ohd *reh*-vah shah-*ah*
	עוד רבע שעה
in half an hour	**od khatsi sha'ah**
	ohd khah-*tsi* shah-*ah*
	עוד חצי שעה
in three-quarters of an hour	**od shloshet riv'ey sha'ah**
	ohd *shloh*-shet riv
	ehy shah-*ah*
	עוד שלושת רבעי שעה

DAYS

Monday	**yom sheni**
	yohm sheh-*nee*
	יום שני
Tuesday	**yom shlishi**
	yohm shlee-*shee*
	יום שלישי
Wednesday	**yom revi'i**
	yohm reh-vee-*ee*
	יום רביעי
Thursday	**yom khamishi**
	yohm khah-mee-*shee*
	יום חמישי
Friday	**yom shishi**
	yohm shee-*shee*
	יום שישי
Saturday	**yom shabat**
	yohm shah-*baht*
	יום שבת
Sunday	**yom rishon**
	yohm ree-*shon*
	יום ראשון
last Monday	**yom sheni she'avar**
	yohm sheh-*nee* sheh-ah-*vahr*
	יום שני שעבר
next Tuesday	**yom shlishi habah**
	yohm shlee-*shee* hah-*bah*
	יום שלישי הבא

on Wednesday	**be-yom revi'i** beh-*yohm* reh-vee-*ee* ביום רביעי
on Thursdays	**biymey khamishi** beey-*mehy* khah-mee-*shee* בימי חמישי
until Friday	**ad yom shishi** ahd yohm shee-*shee* עד יום שישי
until Saturday	**ad shabat** ahd shah-*baht* עד שבת
before Sunday	**lifney yom rishon** leef-*nehy* yom ree-*shon* לפני יום ראשון
before Monday	**lifney yom sheni** leef-*nehy* yom sheh-*nee* לפני יום שני
after Wednesday	**akharey yom revi'i** ah-khah-*rehy* yom reh-vee-*ee* אחרי יום רביעי
after Thursday	**akharey yom khamishi** ah-khah-*rehy* yom khah-mee-*shee* אחרי יום חמישי
the day before yesterday	**shilshom** sheel-*shohm* שלשום
two days ago	**lifney yomayim** lif-*nehy* yoh-*mah*-yim לפני יומיים
yesterday	**etmol** eht-*mohl* אתמול
yesterday morning	**etmol ba-boker** eht-*mohl* bah-*boh*-ker אתמול בבוקר
yesterday afternoon	**etmol akharey ha-tsohorayim** eht-*mohl* ah-khah-*rehy* hah-tsoh hoh-*rah*-yim אתמול אחרי הצהריים
last night	**etmol ba-laylah** eht-*mohl* bah-*lye*-lah אתמול בלילה

today	**ha-yom** hah-*yohm* היום
this morning	**ha-boker** hah-*boh*-ker הבוקר
this afternoon	**hayom akharey hatsohorayim** hah-*yohm* ah-khah-*rehy* hah-tsoh-hoh-*rah*-yim היום אחרי הצהריים
tonight	**ha-laylah** hah-*lye*-lah הלילה
tomorrow	**makhar** mah-*khahr* מחר
tomorrow morning	**makhar ba-boker** mah-*khahr* bah-*boh*-ker מחר בבוקר
tomorrow afternoon	**makhar akharey ha-tsohorayim** mah-*khahr* ah-khah-*rehy* hah-tsoh-hoh-*rah*-yim מחר אחרי הצהריים
tomorrow evening	**makhar ba-erev** mah-*khahr* bah-*eh*-rev מחר בערב
tomorrow night	**makhar ba-laylah** mah-*khahr* bah-*lye*-lah מחר בלילה
the day after tomorrow	**mokhrotayim** mokh-roh-*tah*-yim מחרתיים

MONTHS AND DATES

January	**Yanooar** *yah*-noo-ahr ינואר
February	**Febrooar** *fehb*-roo-ahr פברואר
March	**Mars** mahrs מרס

April	**April**	
	ahp-*reel*	
	אפריל	
May	**May**	
	mye	
	מאי	
June	**Yooni**	
	yoo-nee	
	יוני	
July	**Yooli**	
	yoo-lee	
	יולי	
August	**Ogoost**	
	oh-goost	
	אוגוסט	
September	**September**	
	sehp-*tem*-ber	
	ספטמבר	
October	**Oktober**	
	ohk-*toh*-ber	
	אוקטובר	
November	**November**	
	noh-*vehm*-ber	
	נובמבר	
December	**Detsember**	
	deh-*tsem*-behr	
	דצמבר	
in January	**be-yanooar**	
	beh-*yah*-noo-ahr	
	בינואר	
in September	**be-september**	
	beh-sehp-*tem*-ber	
	בספטמבר	
until February	**ad febrooar**	
	ahd *fehb*-roo-ahr	
	עד פברואר	
until July	**ad yooli**	
	ahd *yoo*-lee	
	עד יולי	
before March	**lifney mars**	
	lif-*nehy* mahrs	
	לפני מרס	

before April	**lifney april** lif-*nehy* ahp-*reel* לפני אפריל
after May	**akharey may** ah-khah-*rehy* mye אחרי מאי
during June	**be-meshekh yooni** beh-*meh*-shekh *yoo*-nee במשך יוני
not before July	**lo lifney yooli** loh lif-*nehy yoo*-lee לא לפני יולי
the beginning of August	**tkhilat ogoost** tkhee-*laht oh*-goost תחילת אוגוסט
the middle of September	**emtsah september** *ehm*-tsah sehp-*tem*-ber אמצע ספטמבר
the end of October	**sof oktober** sohf ohk-*toh*-ber סוף אוקטובר
last month	**ba-khodesh she'avar** bah-*khoh*-desh sheh-ah-*vahr* בחודש שעבר
this month	**ha-khodesh** hah-*khoh*-desh החודש
next month	**ba-khodesh ha-bah** bah-*khoh*-desh hah-*bah* בחודש הבא
in spring	**ba-aviv** bah-ah-*viv* באביב
in summer	**ba-kayits** bah-*kah*-yits בקיץ
in autumn	**ba-stav** bah-*stahv* בסתיו
in winter	**ba-khoref** bah-*khoh*-ref בחורף

this year	**ha-shanah** hah-shah-*nah* השנה
last year	**ba-shanah she-avrah** bah-shah-*nah* sheh-ahv-*rah* בשנה שעברה
next year	**ba-shanah ha-ba'ah** bah-shah-*nah* hah-bah-*ah* בשנה הבאה
in 1992	**be-elef tshah me'ot tish'im oo-shtayim** beh-*eh*-lef *tshah* meh-oht tish-*eem* oo-*shtah*-yim באלף תשע מאות תשעים ושתיים
in 2000	**bi-shnat alpayim** bee-*shnaht* ahl-*pah*-yim בשנת אלפיים
What's the date today?	**Mah ha-ta'arikh ha-yom?** mah hah-tah-ah-*rikh* hah-*yohm* מה התאריך היום?
It's 6th March	**Ha-shishah be-mars** hah-shee-*shah* beh-*mahrs* השישה במארס
12th April	**Ha-shneym asar be-april** hah-*shnehy*m ah-*sahr* beh-ahp-*ril* השנים עשר באפריל
21 August	**ha-esrim ve-ekhad be-ogoost** hah-ess-*rim* veh-eh-*khahd* beh-*oh*-goost העשרים ואחד באוגוסט
23rd April	**ha-esrim oo-shloshah be-april** hah-ess-*rim* oo-shloh-*shah* beh-ahp-*ril* העשרים ושלושה באפריל

HOLIDAYS

- Israel is a Jewish state with a large Muslim, and a small Christian, minority. There are therefore three calendars in use. While the Western calendar is used for most practical purposes, religious and national holidays are determined by Jewish and Muslim calendars.
- Many Israelis consider 1st January a holiday. Here are some other important dates:

1 January	**ha-ekhad be-Yanooar** hah-eh-*khad* beh-*yah*-noo-ahr האחד בינואר	New Year's Day (Christian)
29 November	**ha-esrim ve-tish'ah be-november** hah-ess-*rim* veh-tish-*ah* beh-noh-*vem*-ber העשרים ותשעה בנובמבר	U.N. Declaration in favour of partition and establishment of a Jewish state
25 December	**khag ha-molad** khahg hah-moh-*lahd* חג המולד	Christmas (Christian)

RELIGIOUS FESTIVALS

- The Jewish calendar is lunar. Each month begins with the new moon. Lunar years are some eleven days shorter than solar years, and in order to reconcile to the two systems, every two to three years a month is added to the Jewish year, in a cycle repeated every nineteen years. Jewish religious festivals, therefore, have no exact 'solar' date, but always occur in the same season. New Year's Day (*Rosh ha-hshanah*) is around September, **Khanukah** (the feast of lights) in December, and Passover in April. Independence Day (*yom ha-atsma'oot*) is usually celebrated in May.
- Muslim years are purely lunar, and aren't adjusted to the solar calendar. Islamic festivals move gradually through all the months of the year. The two important festivals are **'ld el-fitr** (the breaking of the fast) when Muslims celebrate the end of *Ramadan*, the month of fasting, and **'ld el-adha** (the sacrifice festival) at the end of the pilgrimage season. The month of *Ramadan* itself is also a time of festivities.

COUNTRIES AND NATIONALITIES

Australia	**Ostralyah**
	oss-*trahl*-yah
	אוסטרליה
Austria	**Ostriyah**
	oss-tree-yah
	אוסטריה
Belgium	**Belgiyah**
	bel-ghee-yah
	בלגיה
Britain	**Britanyah**
	bree-*tahn*-yah
	בריטניה
Canada	**Kanadah**
	kah-nah-dah
	קנדה
Czechoslovakia	**Chekhoslovakyah**
	cheh-khoh-sloh-*vahk*-yah
	צ'כוסלובקיה
East Africa	**Mizrakh Afrikah**
	miz-*rahkh ahf*-ree-kah
	מזרח אפריקה
Egypt	**Mitsrayim**
	mits-*rah*-yim
	מצרים
Eire	**Eyr**
	ehyr
	אייר
England	**Angliyah**
	ahn-glee-yah
	אנגליה
France	**Tsarfat**
	tsahr-*faht*
	צרפת
Germany	**Germanyah**
	Gher-*mahn*-yah
	גרמניה
Greece	**Yavan**
	yah-*vahn*
	יוון
India	**Hodoo**
	hoh-doo
	הודו

Israel	**Yisrael** yiss-rah-*el* ישראל
Italy	**Italyah** ee-*tahl*-yah איטליה
Jordan	**Yarden** yahr-*den* ירדן
Lebanon	**Levanon** leh-vah-*non* לבנון
Luxembourg	**Looksemboorg** *look*-sem-boorg לוקסמבורג
Netherlands	**Holand** *hoh*-lahnd הולנד
New Zealand	**Nyoo Zeeland** nyoo *zee*-lahnd ניו זילנד
Northern Ireland	**Tsfon Irland** tsfohn *eer*-lahnd צפון אירלנד
Pakistan	**Pakistan** pah-kiss-*tahn* פקיסטן
Poland	**Polin** poh-*lin* פולין
Portugal	**Portoogal** por-too-*gahl* פורטוגל
Scotland	**Skotland** *skoht*-lahnd סקוטלנד
South Africa	**Drom Afrikah** drohm *ahf*-ree-kah דרום אפריקה
Spain	**Sfarad** sfah-*rahd* ספרד

Switzerland	**Shvayts**	
	shvahyts	
	שווייץ	
Syria	**Sooryah**	
	soor-yah	
	סוריה	
Turkey	**Toorkiyah**	
	toor-ki-yah	
	תורכיה	
United States	**Artsot ha-brit**	
	ahr-*tsot* hah-*brit*	
	ארצות הברית	
USSR	**Brit ha-moatsot**	
	breet hah-moh-ah-*tsot*	
	ברית המועצות	
Wales	**Weyls**	
	wehyls	
	ויילס	
West Indies	**Jamaykah**	
	jah-*mye*-kah	
	ג׳מייקה	
Yugoslavia	**Yoogoslavyah**	
	yoo-goh-*slahv*-yah	
	יוגוסלביה	

Nationalities

American	**Amerika'i** ah-meh-ree-*kah*-ee אמריקאי
Australian	**Ostrali** oss-*trah*-lee אוסטרלי
British	**Briti** *bree*-tee בריטי
Canadian	**Kanadi** kah-*nah*-dee קנדי
Dutch	**Holandi** hoh-*lahn*-dee הולנדי
Egyptian	**Mitsri** mits-*ree* מצרי
English	**Angli** ahn-*glee* אנגלי
German	**Germani** Gehr-mah-*nee* גרמני
Greek	**Yevani** yeh-vah-*nee* יווני
Indian	**Hodi** *Hoh*-dee הודי
Irish	**Eeri** *ee*-ree אירי
Italian	**Italki** ee-tahl-*kee* איטלקי
Jordanian	**Yardeni** yahr-*deh*-nee ירדני
New Zealander	**Nyoo zeelandi** nyoo zee-*lahn*-dee ניו זילנדי

Pakistani	**Pakistani**
	pah-kiss-*tah*-nee
	פקיסטני
Scots	**Skoti**
	skoh-tee
	סקוטי
South African	**Drom Afrika'i**
	drohm ahf-ree-*kah*-ee
	דרום אפריקה
Spanish	**Sfaradi**
	sfah-rah-*dee*
	ספרדי
Syrian	**Soori**
	soo-ree
	סורי
Welsh	**Welshi**
	well-shee
	ולשי
West Indian	**Mi-Jamaykah**
	mee-jah-*mye*-kah
	מג׳מייקה
Yugoslav	**Yoogoslavi**
	yoo-goh-*slah*-vee
	יוגוסלבי

CONVERSION TABLES

Read the centre column of these tables from right to left to convert
from metric to U.S. measures and from left to right to convert from
U.S. to metric, e.g., 5 litres = 10.57 pints; 5 pints = 2.37 liters.

pints		litres		gallons		litres
2.11	1	0.47		0.26	1	3.79
4.23	2	0.95		0.53	2	7.57
6.34	3	1.42		0.79	3	11.36
8.46	4	1.89		1.06	4	15.15
10.57	5	2.37		1.32	5	18.94
12.68	6	2.84		1.58	6	22.72
14.80	7	3.31		1.85	7	26.51
16.91	8	3.78		2.11	8	30.30
19.03	9	4.26		2.38	9	34.08

miles		kilometres
0.62	1	1.61
1.24	2	3.22
1.86	3	4.83
2.49	4	6.44
3.11	5	8.05
3.73	6	9.66
4.35	7	11.27
4.97	8	12.87
5.59	9	14.48

A quick way to convert kilometres to miles: divide by 8 and multiply by 5. To convert miles to kilometres: divide by 5 and multiply by 8.

fahrenheit (°F)	centigrade (°C)	lbs/ sq in	k/ sq cm
212°	100° boiling point	18	1.3
100°	38°	20	1.4
98.4°	36.9° body temperature	22	1.5
86°	30°	25	1.7
77°	25°	29	2.0
68°	20°	32	2.3
59°	15°	35	2.5
50°	10°	36	2.5
41°	5°	39	2.7
32°	0° freezing point	40	2.8
14°	−10°	43	3.0
−4°	−20°	45	3.2
		46	3.2
		50	3.5
		60	4.2

To convert °C to °F: divide by 5, multiply by 9 and add 32.
To convert °F to °C: take away 32, divide by 9 and multiply by 5.

CLOTHING SIZES

Remember – always try on clothes before buying.
Clothing sizes are usually unreliable.

women's dresses and suits

Europe	38	40	42	44	46	48
UK	32	34	36	38	40	42
USA	10	12	14	16	18	20

men's suits and coats

Europe	46	48	50	52	54	56
UK and USA	36	38	40	42	44	46

men's shirts

Europe	36	37	38	39	41	42	43
UK and USA	14	14½	15	15½	16	16½	17

socks

Europe	38-39	39-40	40-41	41-42	42-43
UK and USA	9½	10	10½	11	11½

shoes

Europe	34	35½	36½	38	39	41	42	43	44	45
UK	2	3	4	5	6	7	8	9	10	11
USA	3½	4½	5½	6½	7½	8½	9½	10½	11½	12½

Do it yourself

Some notes on the language

- A definitive grammar of Hebrew is not the purpose of this section. Just Enough Hebrew offers a simple short cut to day-to-day communication in Israel. The 'do it yourself' section seeks to go a little further, and to explain some of the basic rules of the language. It offers a more efficient tool, enabling you to formulate innumerable sentences of your own.
- There is no phonetic transcription in this section. Partly because it would get in the way of the explanation, and partly because you have to do it yourself at this stage if you are serious. Work out the pronunciation from all the earlier examples in the book.

NOUNS

- All nouns in Hebrew are either masculine or feminine, irrespective of whether they refer to living beings or to inanimate objects.
- Many feminine nouns end with the vowel . . **ah**, or with a **t**. There are many exceptions to this rule, but it would be a safe bet to assume that nouns with these endings are feminine.

masculine:		feminine:	
boy – yeled		girl – yald*ah*	
book – sefer		lamp – menor*ah*	
day – yom		train – rakeve*t*	
tree – ets		promenade – tayele*t*	

- Knowing the gender of a given noun could help you build a sentence, and is relevant especially in these two cases:

1 In the **plural**. Most masculine nouns end with . . **im**. Most feminine nouns end with . . **ot**.

	singular	plural
masculine: boy	yeled	yelad*im*
feminine: lamp	menorah	menor*ot*

2 When followed by an **adjective**. Like nouns, adjectives have masculine or feminine endings, according to the nouns they describe:

		noun	**adjective**
masculine:	a good boy	yeled	tov
	a big tree	ets	gadol
feminine:	a good girl	yald*ah*	tov*ah*
	a big car	mekhoni*t*	gdol*ah*

● Here are several examples of masculine and feminine nouns, and their plural form:

	masculine	feminine	plural
an address		ktovet	ktov*ot*
an apple	tapooahkh		tapookh*im*
a beer		birah	bir*ot*
a bill	kheshbon		kheshbon*ot**
a bus	otoboos		otoboos*im*
a deer		ayalah	ayal*ot*
a hat	kovah		kova'*im*
a key	mafte'akh		maftekh*ot**
a menu	tafrit		tafrit*im*
a newspaper	eeton		eeton*im*
a receipt		kabalah	kabal*ot*
a restaurant		miss'adah	miss'ad*ot*
a roll		lakhmaniyah	lakhmaniy*ot*
a room	kheder		khadar*im*
a telephone	telefon		telefon*im*

● You can get along easily without knowing the right gender of a noun or an adjective. However, if you listen to what people say, you will soon pick up which is the correct one to use.

Using the words in the table above, practise saying these sentences in Hebrew:

Have you got a receipt?	yesh lekhah kabalah?
a telephone?	yesh lekhah . . .
I'd like a roll	ani rotseh lakhmaniyah
some rolls	ani rotseh kamah . . .
Where can I get a newspaper?	eyfoh efshar le-hassig . . .
a hat?	eyfoh efshar le-hassig . . .
Is there a key?	yesh mafte'akh?
a telephone?	yesh . . .?
an apple?	yesh . . .?
a restaurant?	yesh . . .?
a room?	yesh . . .?
Are there any rooms?	yesh khadarim?
any newspapers?	yesh . . .?
any keys?	yesh . . .?

Now try to make up more sentences along these lines using other vocabulary in the book.

*These are some examples of exceptions to the rule, where 'masculine' nouns get 'feminine' endings.

A/THE

- There is no indefinite article (a/an) in Hebrew. Thus, 'a boy' is simply *yeled*; 'a house' is just *bayit*. One can also choose, in certain cases, to refer to 'one boy' (*yeled ekhad*) or 'one house' (*bayit ekhad*) meaning 'a certain boy' or 'a certain house'.
- The definite article (the) is *ha-*. It is added at the beginning of the word, and forms an integral part of it in writing. It does not change according to gender or number:

	singular	plural
the boy	ha-yeled	ha-yeladim
the girl	ha-yaldah	ha-yeladot
the duck	ha-barvaz	ha-barvazim
the book	ha-sefer	ha-sfarim

Using the words in the tables above, practise saying these sentences in Hebrew:

Have you seen the boy?	Ra'itah et ha-yeled?
the girl?	Ra'itah et . . .?
Have you found the key?	Matsatah et . . .?
the bill?	Matsatah et . . .?
the address?	Matsatah et . . .?
the book?	Matsatah et . . .?
Give me the receipt	Ten li et ha-kabalah
the bill	Ten li et
the keys	Ten li et
the apple	Ten li et
Where is the duck?	Eyfoh . . .?
the restaurant?	Eyfoh . . .?
the hat?	Eyfoh . . .?
Where are the books?	Eyfoh ha-sfarim?
the rooms?	Eyfoh . . .?
the telephones?	Eyfoh . . .?
the apples?	Eyfoh . . .?

YESH/EYN

- There is no word, in the English sense, for 'have' in Hebrew. Instead the word **yesh** (literally, 'existent' or 'there is') and the word **eyn** (pronounced *ehn*, literally, 'non-existent' or 'there isn't') are used. These words always precede the noun.

A question format would be:

| is there a book? | **yesh sefer?** |
| are there any books? | **yesh sfarim?** |

In reply you will hear:

| **yesh** | there is/there are |
| **eyn** | there isn't/there aren't (any) |

Practise saying these sentences in Hebrew (remembering that to say 'some/any' use just the word on its own):

Have you got some coffee?	**yesh lekhah kafeh?**
some wine?	**Y . . . yayin?**
some bread?	**. . . lekhem?**
Is there any water?	**Yesh mayim?**
any cheese?	**. . . gvinah?**
any tea?	**. . . teh?**
Are there any keys?	**. . . maftekhot?**
Isn't there any beer?	**Eyn birah?**
any water?	**. . . mayim?**
any wine?	**. . . yayin?**
Aren't there any newspapers?	**. . . eetonim?**

HELPING OTHERS

You can help yourself with phrases such as:

I'd like (a roll)	**Anee rotseh (lakhmaniyah)**
I need (a receipt)	**Anee tsarikh (kabalah)**
Can I get (a cup of coffee)?	**Efshar lekabel (koss kafeh)?**

If you come across a compatriot having trouble making himself or herself understood, you should be able to speak on their behalf. (A pronunciation guide is provided from here on, to help you with the unfamiliar parts of each phrase.)

The word for **he** is 'hoo'. The word for **she** is 'hee'.

- Note that there are different verb forms for 'he' and 'she'.

He'd like (a sandwich)	**Hoo rotseh (sendvich)** hoo roh-*tseh* (*send*-vitch)
She'd like (a beer)	**Hee rotsah (birah)** hee roh-*tsah* (*bee*-rah)
Where can he get (some tea)?	**Eyfoh hoo yakhol lekabel (teh)?** ehy-*foh* hoo yah-*khol* leh-kah-*bel* (teh)
Where can she get (a sandwich)	**Eyfoh hee yekholah lekabel (sendvich)?** ehy-*foh* hee yeh-khoh-*lah* leh-kah-*bel* (*send*-vitch)
He needs (a receipt)	**Hoo tsarikh (kabalah)** hoo tsah-*rikh* (kah-bah-*lah*)
She needs (a ticket)	**Hee tsreekhah (kartis)** hee tsree-*khah* (kahr-*tiss*)

- You can also help a couple or a group if they are having difficulties.
- The word for 'they' is **hem**. There is also a feminine 'they' – **hen**. It is used only when 'they' are all of feminine gender.
- To make the plural form of the verb, add . . . **im** (or . . . **ot** when the feminine gender is concerned) to the 'he/she' form. If the verb ends with a vowel, it is usually omitted:

he needs – **hoo tsarikh** hoo tsah-*rikh*	they need – (m.) **hem tsrikhim** hem tree-*khim*
she needs – **hee tsrikhah** hee tsree-*khah*	they need – (f.) **hen tsrikhot** hen tsree-*khot*

They'd like (some cheese)	**Hem rotsim (gveenah)** hem roh-*tsim* (gvee-*nah*)
Where can they get (some aspirin)?	**Eyfoh hem yekholim le-kabel (aspirin)?** ehy-*foh* hem yeh-khoh-*lim* leh-kah-*bel* (ahs-pee-*rin*)
They drink (wine)	**Hem shotim (yayin)** hem shoh-*tim* (*yah*-yin)
They (the ladies) ask (what the address is)	**Hen sho'alot (mah ha-ktovet)** hen shoh-ah-*lot* (*mah* bah-*ktoh*-vet)

What about the two of you? No problem. The word for 'we' is **anakhnoo** (ah-*nahkh*-noo). The verb ending stays the same as in 'they' – just add . . . **im** (or . . . **ot**) to the singular form:

We'd like (some wine)	**Anakhnoo rotsim (yayin)**
	ah-*nahkh*-noo roh-*tsim yah*-yin
Where can we get (some water)?	**Eyfoh anakhnoo yekholim le-kabel (mayim)?**
	ehy-foh ah-*nahkh*-noo yeh-khoh-*lim* leh-kah-*bel* (*mah*-yim)
We are drinking (beer)	**Anakhnoo shotim (birah)**
	ah-*nahkh*-noo shoh-*tim* (*bee*-rah)

USEFUL WORDS

Try memorizing these six useful words:

I want/need	(m) **anee tsarikh**
	ah-*nee* tsah-*rikh*
	(f) **anee tsrikhah**
	ah-*nee* tsree-*khah*
I don't want/need	(m) **anee lo tsarikh**
	ah-*nee loh* tsah-*rikh*
	(f) **anee lo tsrikhah**
	ah-*nee loh* tsree-*khah*
I know	(m) **anee yode'a**
	ah-*nee* yoh-*deh*-ah
	(f) **anee yoda'at**
	ah-*nee* yoh-*dah*-aht
I don't know	(m) **anee lo yode'a**
	ah-*nee* loh yoh-*deh*-ah
	(f) **anee lo yoda'at**
	ah-*nee* loh yoh-*dah*-aht
I understand	(m) **anee mevin**
	ah-*nee* meh-*vin*
	(f) **anee mevinah**
	ah-*nee* meh-vee-*nah*
I don't understand	(m) **anee lo mevin**
	ah-*nee* loh meh-*vin*
	(f) **anee lo mevinah**
	ah-*nee* loh meh-vee-*nah*

MORE PRACTICE

Here are some more Hebrew names of things. See how many
different sentences you can make up, using the various points of
information given earlier in this section.

		singular	plural
1	ashtray	ma'aferah	ma'aferot
2	bag	tik	tikim
3	bank	bank	bankim
4	car	mekhonit	mekhoniyot
5	cigarette	sigaryah	sigaryot
6	egg	beytsah	beytsim
7	garage (repairs)	moosakh	moosakhim
8	glove	kfafah	kfafot
9	grapefruit	eshkolit	eshkoliyot
10	ice-cream	glidah	glidot
11	knife	sakin	sakinim
12	melon	melon	melonim
13	passport	darkon	darkonim
14	plate	tsalakhat	tsalakhot
15	postcard	glooyah	glooyot
16	salad	salat	satatim
17	shoe	na'al	na'alayim
18	stamp	bool	boolim
19	station	takhanah	takhanot
20	street	rekhov	rekhovot
21	suitcase	mizvadah	mizvadot
22	telephone	telefon	telefonim
23	ticket	kartiss	kartissim

Index